It Happened in Prince Edward County

It Happened in Prince Edward County

by

D. K. Redner

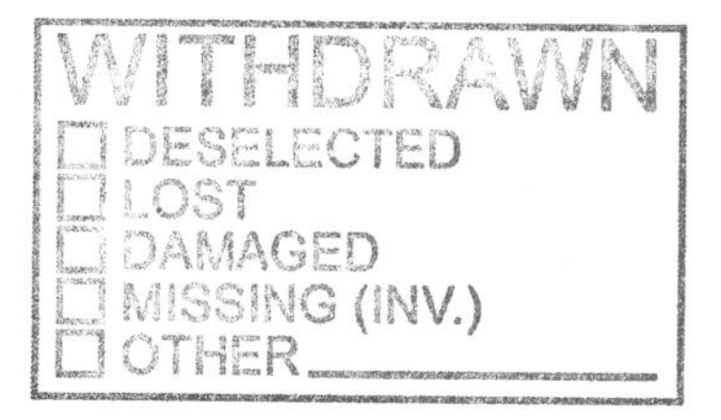

MIKA PUBLISHING COMPANY
Belleville, Ontario
1976

The material appearing in this book was first published by the *Picton Gazette* and is reprinted with permission.

It Happened in Prince Edward County

ISBN 0-919303-05-6

Printed and bound in Canada

Picture on cover: Wellington Main Street

Contents

Introduction 7
The Redner Family 9
The Story of Rossmore Village 13
The Dempseys 17
The DeLongs 20
The Pulvers 22
The Brickmans 25
Oscar Burley's Reminiscences 30
The Anderson Family 36
Herb Love's Reminiscences 40
The Moy Family 45
The Peck Family and Albury 48
The Doxsee Family 56
The Sprague Family 59
The Sprague Telephone System 63
Main Duck Island — Days of Rum Runners 68
King Cole Rules His Island Kingdom 71
Eatonville 74
The Conger Family 86
The Conger Chapel 90
Roblin's Mills 94
The Village of Wellington 104
The Files 116
Rednersville Lady of Ninety 120
In Retrospect 124

The Country Store, Rednersville. (Drawing by Donnah Cameron.)

Introduction

This book contains a collection of stories and historical articles written by D. K. Redner, a native of Prince Edward County, some twenty years ago for the *Picton Gazette.* At that time, Mr. Redner interviewed many of the old-time county residents and gathered the material which otherwise might have been lost. A reader of the *Gazette* back then wrote a letter to the editor, and this is what he said: "One hundred years from now there will be people who will be thanking God that a man named D. K. Redner took time to write the history of the Pioneers . . ."

Most of the articles have been published between 1951 and 1954, and we are grateful to the president of the *Picton Gazette,* Mr. J. Cembal, for allowing us to reprint some of the interesting accounts dealing with people and places in the County.

Much has happened since the author first wrote his stories. Properties have changed hands, houses have disappeared, and businesses have closed their doors. We have not attempted to update the facts to the present day. It is left to the reader to reminisce and fill in some of the events of the last twenty years or so.

D. K. Redner. (Photo by Lloyd E. Thompson.)

The Redner Family

During my wanderings around the county in quest of material for my articles, I have often been asked by one person or another why I did not write an article on my own family. The question is one that deserves a better answer than is usually given, for rather than admit my ignorance of the family background I usually give them some off-hand reply which might make them smile but does not give them the slightest reason to suspect that the fact of the matter simply is that there is no established link between the time of their leaving the homeland in Europe and the time of the first Redner settlement on the shores of the Bay of Quinte — a settlement which in due time became known as Rednersville. The latter was at one time a thriving settlement but with the coming of the years and the changing of the times it has degenerated into just another of those sleeply little country villages whose stores a century ago boasted more activity than the whole village today. Those were the days of the cracker barrel and the kerosene lamps and also when the farmers for miles around brought their butter and eggs to the country store and exchanged them for groceries and other necessities of life. That was the time too, when the menfolk of the whole community sat around the old wood stove in the corner and not only gossiped about the weather, but also passed judgement on the questions of the day.

The Redners made a real start toward a thriving village and it is regrettable that their efforts have been nullified through both progress and fire.

Several years ago it was my privilege to do an article on the oldest member of the family in the village at the time — William Henry — but though he had seen the advent of ninety summers, could tell little of the history of the famliy beyond their settlement in Prince Edward County.

My mother has in her possession an exceedingly old Dutch Bible which was brought over by people by the name of Riddener so, as time passed, we are first of all led to believe that changes were made on at least one occasion in the family name.

I had always understood from my father that the Redners came from Holland but now after many years of search and investigation we are not yet certain whether their abode was within the German border of Holland or within the Dutch border of Germany. Only a few miles of territory in this case might completely change the whole background as well as the nationality of the family.

There always seemed to be one point that my father seemed clear on, however, and that was that the Redners had come as United Empire Loyalists from Pennsylvania. He never gave any proof of his theory nor did he give the slightest inclination as to the source of his information; he just told me and it stayed with me through the years.

He passed on in 1930 and it was well to twenty years before I took up the torch in earnest and became interested in not only our own family history but anything in the County of Prince Edward that had a historical background.

In the meantime a cattle buyer came our way from a small town in Northern Pennsylvania by the name of Wellsboro and this man awakened an enthusiasm in my soul to make what might be termed a pilgrimage to that place because he gave me the information that there were Redners around the part of the country where he came from. In a flash I made up my mind to do one thing — I was going to Wellsboro even if it took years to achieve such an object of my dreams. I steadfastly refused to say or even think it would never take place and one summer brought the realization of that determination.

We arrived in Wellsboro about five-thirty. It wasn't late as daylight went but the stores closed at five so I scanned the R's in the phone book, visited the local newspaper office and inquired at a couple of garages. The result had failure written all over it in large letters. I was profoundly disappointed. There was not a single trace of any Redners either in the town or the surrounding country. I tried once more and a visit to a third garage brought a ray of hope. One of its employees knew of a man by the name of Redner — Paul Redner. Was that the name of the chap I was looking for? Immediately I answered "Yes". I did not go so far as to tell him the exact truth for by that time any person by the name of Redner was on the wanted list and I grasped at such a tid-bit of information like a drowning man would reach for a straw. Paul

Redner didn't live in Wellsboro but in Westfield he thought — about twenty miles back and only a short distance from our route down. In little over half an hour we were in the edge of Westfield only to find that he ran a service station at Knoxville six miles back the road we had driven over but a few minutes before.

Without a doubt Paul Redner was the most surprised man in Knoxville that afternoon. We talked for perhaps half an hour and he told me of another member of the family who lived a few miles away near a little village called Tioga still in Pennsylvania. His name was Henry and his father's name had been William — not at all uncommon names in our own branch of the family. He told us about still more Redners in Elmira so after spending the night in the village we continued our quest, arriving in Elmira about 10:30 on an exceedingly warm Tuesday morning. Elmira, which boasts a population of approximately seventy thousand is across the border in the state of New York and it was here that my fullest ambition was realized. This proved to be the hub of the Redner settlement purported to be in Northern Pennsylvania. Once within the boundaries of the city I lost no time in finding that three were listed in the telephone book — Fred, Walter and W. R. The names meant absolutely nothing to me except in the years gone by another Fred Redner lived two farms away from our own. My wife and daughter, Betty, were my companions and, leaving them on a window shopping tour of the main street, I started out on foot for Riverside Avenue.

A charming young lady opened the door and immediately made me feel one hundred per cént at home. Her husband, Willis, was an advertising salesman for the firm of Brown and Bigelow and was not at home at the time but from her I learned much. First of all her name was Betty and she had, before her marriage, been a school-teacher. The Redners were on the increase in that part of the world, she said, and most people of the name had moderate families. She and her husband had a family of four. There were enough who were either Redners or had been to make possible the holding of a family picnic each summer and here I was sitting in the front room of the very person who was contributing much to its success. She was, to use a single word, its secretary. She used the telephone to call her husband's Uncle Walter who was at the time on holiday from Remington Rand. He lived in the same part of the city and arrived in a very few minutes. By an exceedingly strange co-incidence he and his wife had a daughter Joan who was training for a nurse in a Philadelphia hospital. Our own daughter Joan was at that very time completing her period of training for the same profession in Kingston. The same kind of a surprise awaited him also because several of them had been in Canada on more occasions than one and, like myself, had always looked through every means at their disposal but had failed to discover the least trace of the name and had come to the common conclusion that any Redners who might have migrated to Ontario had either become extinct or there never had veen any in the first place. Although the village of Rednersville is marked on more than one road map of New York State they had failed to notice it and had all but eliminated the possibility of the existence of the name anywhere in Ontario.

The Redners in Elmira seemed to be much more clannish than those in Rednersville. Each winter they have a weekly social evening and play games and further their already happy associations. In Rednersville they seldom take time for more than a friendly chat of a few minutes duration. In Elmira the yearly picnic is either inside the city or near by and is not only looked forward to but largely attended.

View of the old bridge crossing the Bay from Rossmore to Belleville

The Story of Rossmore Village Told by W. Belnap

The Belnaps, like a lot of our present-day settlers, are of United Empire Loyalist stock but of French descent. William Belnap, Sr., came from near Syracuse and settled at Point Anne at the time of the influx of U.E.L. settlers to this country. He dropped dead on the street in Belleville one day during a cholera epidemic which occurred some time in the fore part of the nineteenth century, but left a family consisting of three sons and five daughters, the boys making history by marrying three sisters. The boys were David, Daniel and John.

DAVID moved from Point Anne to Rossmore and had a family of four boys and two girls. Walter, Manley and Jim have passed on while William, the subject of our sketch, lives on the bay side of front street in Rossmore. One girl, Mrs. Ed. Cronkright, died in 1920 with the flu and Mrs. Lester Simmons lives in Thorold. William Belnap married Martha Hebert on April 23, 1892, the marriage ceremony being performed by Rev. Sexsmith at Roblin's Mills. That was a memorable day for one other couple also as it was the occasion of a double wedding, Frank Thompson and Susie Duke being married at the same time.

The Belnaps had two girls and one boy. Claude, better known to most of the present-day generation as Pete, had a barber shop in Belleville. Mrs. Bernard Boulter of Rossmore is a daughter while the other girl, Una, married Ben Foster, son of a veterinary in Belleville. Both these people died within three days of each other in Windsor in 1920 with the flu, and their two children, Jack and Gena, came to live with their grandfather and grandmother. Jack spent six years, three and a half months in the army, most of which was overseas. He was through the North African campaign and was wounded twice in the same day in Holland. For bravery on this occasion he was awarded the military medal and later promoted to company sergeant major.

BILL BELNAP received his early education at the old school

house in Rossmore and after it was closed continued to go to Massassaga. The old saw mill was running to full capacity then and the population of the village was between twelve and thirteen hundred. The old school in the village was down in the edge of the mill yard and was built of pine lumber sawed at the Eagle mill, as it was called. When the number of scholars was the highest James Carpenter Howell, cousin of Wellington Howell of the second concession of our township, taught one hundred and twenty-five pupils in one room and received a salary of three hundred dollars per annum.

After the mill closed down Rossmore became almost a ghost town and its school was closed, the children being sent to Massassaga. The building was sold to Edward Gerow who moved it up near where the church is now and used it for a cooperage shop. He afterward sold it to Allan Herrington and with some alterations it still stands as the machine shed to the west of the barn on the Herrington farm.

When a boy, Bill's father used to work for Elias Wallbridge in the winter-time and lived in a house on the back end of the farm to look after the young cattle which the Wallbridges owned, as their main farm was not large enough to accommodate them. A fair sized log house had been built to go with the barn where the young cattle were always kept in the off pasture season. Elias Wallbridge was the son of Shelly and father of Ernest, Lewis, James, Fred and Ben and also Helen and Mrs. Fred Morgan. Part of the family is no longer with us but they lived at that time on the farm now owned by R. B. McCulloch, a lawyer in the neighbouring city. Bill and his father drew up the year's wood with a team of oxen.

In the summer time they fished. The Belnaps have always been noted for being fishermen and in those days the fishing was good. The bay was full of all kinds of nets during season and the catch of whitefish netted them as high as a ton at one lift and the nets were drawn up as often as the fishermen could get time to get to them — sometimes as often as three or four times a day. Herring, Pike, Perch and Bullheads were also caught in quantity. The herring and whitefish were cleaned, sugar-cured and packed in half barrels and sold for five dollars a barrel of one hundred pounds. They were shipped from the local dock to Oswego while the rest of the catch was marketed mostly in New York and Buffalo.

Rossmore in the nineties boasted three hotels. Ed. Gerow ran one which was situated just east of where the church now stands — the Rossmore House — which like the other two sold beer and whisky but in addition had a pool room. Captain Willie Gerow ran another one which he built to take the place of a very old building down by the ferry dock. The old hotel through age had become unfit for further use so he built the large brick house across the road from the bridge lookout and operated it for a number of years. A third — The Eagle — was situated on a lot including part of the Argo gas station and extending northeastward to include the ground where Ted Gerow's house stands. This was owned by Andrew Hebert but was run for some time by his son Frank who was Mrs. Belnap's father.

The only traffic to Belleville at that time was by ferry boat, and the first of these on the run across the bay was the *Prince Edward* captained by a man named Gillett. After a rather brief period of operation the boat was condemned and the *Mary Ethel* took over the run. Captain James Anderson had a franchise to carry passengers and freight from Anderson's dock, on Ernest Teney's farm, straight across to the Hastings side so he had only to take his boat and go to work a couple or three miles further down the bay. It could carry seven teams or rigs on each side and was operated by a steam engine which burned cordwood. Its fire box could take several four-foot sticks without difficulty. It had a remarkable capacity for ice-breaking and has been known to break the ice on its trip across while a team of horses were driven only a few feet away. Captain Anderson became involved in some sort of a dispute with the City of Belleville and took his boat off the run but it was replaced by the *Alberta* brought up from Deseronto and operated by Captain Jake Rathbun. The *Alberta* was a smaller boat than the *Mary Ethel* but served the traffic until the completion of the bridge in 1890.

The village had three grocery stores. Johnny Laird kept one where Thompson's gas station is but afterward sold it to Frank Hebert. Peter Martin Frederick kept another where the approach to the bridge now is and the building had to be moved to make the right-of-way to the bridge, while the third was run by Peter W. Friar in the west end of the village. It burned down and was never rebuilt.

The old sawmill was situated half a mile east of where the gas station now is on Highway No. 14 and when first started was set up on a little island. It was first run by a man by the name of Froman who sold it lated to Page and Company. A depression hit the country and business suffered a general recession so the lumber mill was closed down but it was opend some time later by the Rathbun Company who in the meantime had purchased it from its former owners. The logs for the mill were cut in the north country and floated down the Trent and Moira Rivers. When they reached the river mouth in either case they were fastened into booms and towed to their destination by a tug. The Frenchmen, brought up for the purpose, were the only ones skilled enough to ride the logs but local men, including on one occasion Bill Belnap, tailed the run and loosened any logs that might happen to get stuck on any kind of shoal or on shore.

Oswego was the biggest market for the lumber and it was a common sight to look toward the wharf and see seven or eight schooners and tow barges at a single time being loaded with lumber for export. The barges were usually towed by the tug *Al Summers* under Captain Blanchard. It was an extremely powerful little craft and was capable of pulling an immense load. The lumber was loaded by hand labour for which was paid the very large sum of twenty cents an hour. The mill employed one hundred to one hundred and seventy-five men when operating at capacity and the employees were paid a dollar a day for regular work.

The post office in Rossmore was kept by Walt Post in a house near where Fred Juby's cottage now is. The mail was brought from Belleville on the ferry and taken on to Roblin's Mills by stage driver for a period of time by George Tice, father of George the auctioneer, and also by Irvine Coleman.

* * *

The bridge was surveyed in 1888 by government engineers and the contract for its construction was let to a Belleville firm, G. and J. Brown. They ran a foundry in the city. The contract was sublet by them into different lots and Alfred and Lear built the cribwork for the piers. Each crib was filled with piles and covered with concrete and eight-inch timbers to make the top level. Then it was filled to the top of the crib with stone brought up from Point Anne. The cement used was brought from England in barrels lined with paper and the steel was imported from Scotland.

The new bridge was built by Frontenac Construction Co. and was opened for traffic in 1922.

The Dempseys

The Dempseys are of Irish descent, having migrated from Northern Ireland to Vermont and like so many more of our people at the present time have their name enrolled on the list of United Empire Loyalists who came to Adolphustown before their subsequent removal to Prince Edward County. The family spent two years in that place and then came to Ameliasburgh somewhere around the same time as six other pioneer families, the Weeses, the Mikels, the Pecks, the Scamerhorns, the Shears and the Alleys.

The first Dempsey settlement was on lot 90 to the west of the side road carrying the family name and not far from the bay shore. The farm remained in the Dempsey name until a few years ago when Fred sold it to a Dutch farmer. Across the front road — that is the road running from Rednersville to Carrying Place — Harry lived for many years until he met a tragic end when he lost his life in a fire which destroyed his home during the Christmas season of 1949. His son Gordon now lives on the same land on the north side of the highway and across the sideroad from the first Dempsey log house. Two other sons, Donald and Charles also live on the bay shore road and a nephew, Allan lives in Rednersville.

Thomas Dempsey was the original settler and all the people by that name in the township today trace their ancestry to that one man. The tombstone erected in his memory may still be seen in Albury Cemetery about thirty feet directly behind the church.

Herb Dempsey was born on the farm where he now lives but not in the same house — the old house being situated on the crossroad between the second and third concessions and it forms the woodhouse where he and his son Morley live at the present time. His father moved that old house in the winter time when, after getting it on skids it was drawn to its destination with eight teams of oxen. Herb had two brothers, Aaron and Spurgeon. Aaron lived in a house also situated on the same crossroad but the two houses were not there at the same time.

Wellington Loveless married the daughter of Freeman Burley and on their marriage the latter, as a dowry, gave to his daughter twenty acres of land on the third with the promise of the deed as soon as they completed the building of a house. When the young couple had completed their share of the agreement the deed was not forthcoming, so Herb's father Thomas, who had been named after the original settler, purchased an additional twenty-five acres in the sideroad and consequently bought the house from Wellington Loveless and his wife as they refused to live in it after not receiving the deed as promised. The moving of that house stands out as a very unique event in the history of moving buildings for it is the only one that I have ever heard of that was moved entirely by man power. Logs of equal size were cut to be used as rollers and holes were bored equal distances apart both in length and circumference. Iron bars were then used to turn the fore and aft logs and the house was moved perhaps a quarter of a mile in this way. Forty men gave their assistance to the undertaking. Herb was nine years old at the time. Not so many years back — perhaps three or four — the house was again sold and moved to the fourth concession where Frank Keene had lost his house by fire a short time previously.

Thomas Dempsey lived on the front road until he was forty-five years old during which time he worked one hundred and fifty acres in partnership with his brother-in-law, John Onderdonk who had married Mary Jane, his only sister. The two men had in addition two lots of fifty acres each, one on the third and the other part of the farm now occupied by Bruce Hennesey and his son Ralph on the second. During this time the two partners hired additional labour at seeding and harvest time and to make shorter work of the job in the concessions they boarded with a man by the name of John Robinson who, along with his wife, lived in the house on what was then and is now the Dempsey farm. All food was furnished by the men hiring the work done and the only rent paid by the Robinsons was the cooking for the men which Mrs. Robinson did at the two busy seasons of the year. John Robinson worked for Simon DeLong who lived where Truman Ferguson is now. When Thomas was forty-five years old the partners divided the business, the Dempseys moving out to the concession and the Onderdonks remaining on the farm at the foot of Onderdonk's hill — the farm which on John's death was inherited by his son Rice.

Herb married Ada Cunningham from the front road below

Rednersville. She was the daughter of Henry Cunningham and Hulda Redner and sister of Mrs. Hiram Adams who still lives on the farm which is operated by her son Harry. For three years after Herb's marriage he lived with his father-in-law but when his younger brother Spurgeon married and left home he returned to the farm on the third from which Thomas passed on when Herb was thirty-two years old. With the exception of those three years on the front he has spent all his efforts on the farm where he now resides.

After his return to the old home he and his brother Aaron pooled their resources and worked two farms with one set of implements, an arrangement which continued until Aaron sold his interest to Herb who along with that purchase eventually increased his acreage to two hundred and fifty. His wife passed on in 1917 leaving behind one son Morley whose first wife, Pearl Whaley, died in 1921, and his second last autumn. Bessie Hillman left one daughter, Betty who married Bryan Cronk.

Rednersville Church erected 1849. (Drawing by Donnah Cameron.)

The DeLongs

The years following Confederation found the DeLongs the biggest land owners in Ameliasburgh. William DeLong was a man of marked business ability and at one time owned three hundred acres on the third and four hundred on the second. The latter holdings consisted of the two farms where Eldon Adams and his son Art now live and Jack Waterhouse and his son Gordon. Each of those farms extended further to the south — in fact right to the third concession but with the passing of the years a section of each was sold and that land is now owned by George Stinson and the Files. Then the same man owned another three hundred acres which included the File farm on the south side of the third.

WILLIAM DELONG started for Belleville one day and while on his way down the front road was thrown from his buggy somewhere in the vicinity of where William Bedford now lives, and as a result died soon after of a broken neck. His estate, accordingly, was divided among his children, his daughters receiving two lots of fifty acres, Will the farm where the Waterhouses are, Havelock the Adams farm and Fred the remainder.

The hundred acres left to the girls was sold to a man by the name of Orville Carter who was a carriage maker for St. Charles in Belleville for many years. He had given his wife a specified weekly allowance through the years and had never asked any questions. One day he made the remark that if he had the money he would buy that hundred acres from the DeLong estate. His wife surprised him greatly by the information that she had the money which she had saved from her housekeeping allowance and if he thought it advisable to buy the land they would buy it. The deal was made and Herb Dempsey and his brother, Aaron worked the farm for three years, after which the Carters moved out from the city and lived in the stone house now owned by the Files. In addition to their farming enterprise Orville Carter worked part time in Sam Allen's carriage factory in Roblin's Mills. He later traded land with Fred DeLong and from the latter the Files acquired the property.

WILL DELONG married Arvilla Roblin, sister of Delbert and Theodore, and had to build a house to replace an old one on his recently acquired farm. His wife's father agreed to furnish it after it was finished but he built such a large one that Mr. Roblin would not fulfill his promise. The cost was so large that it was the means of the property passing from the DeLong hands. Years later part of it was destroyed by fire and the remainder was rebuilt and that portion is much larger than houses are built today.

HAVELOCK, the third member of the family, never married. He worked his farm for several years and lived alone but eventually rented it to Jimmy Glenn who afterward moved to the township of Seymour.

Havelock DeLong eventually mortgaged his farm and with the money built the hotel in Roblin's Mills. The Marsden House did a thriving business when the village had much more to commend it as a prosperous hamlet than it has today.

Mr. and Mrs. Herb Pulver with three grandchildren.

The Pulvers

"On December 12, 1900, a very pretty wedding took place at the home of the bride's parents, Mr. and Mrs. Walter Pymer, of the 5th Concession of Hillier, when Miss Emma Pymer was united in marriage to Mr. Herbert Pulver of Ameliasburgh. In the middle of the afternoon the bride and groom left for Trenton amid showers of rice. They intend spending a week with relatives in Western Ontario. Mr. and Mrs. Pulver may be seen hereafter on the Pulver homestead in the "Gore" between the first and second concession of Ameliasburgh."

The above is an excerpt from *The Gazette* carrying news of the times of fifty years ago. Communities and the world in general have undergone drastic changes since those times but *The Gazette* is still the family paper, the Gore is still the Gore and the original holdings of the Pulvers have increased through hard work and good management from one farm to three.

The Pymer home was the farm afterward owned by the late David Lambert, but the buildings were burned some years back and the land has now been absorbed by neighbouring farmers.

The Pulver farm was originally granted to "John Rush (and I quote from the crown deed) of the township of Ameliasburgh in the County of Prince Edward in the midland district, yeoman, son of Martin Rush of the same place and U. E. Loyalist, and to his heirs and affigns (assigns) forever two hundred acres". A detailed description of its location is technical and unnecessary but the land stretched from and included the bay frontage now occupied by Harold Hitchon to the base line where is situated the Pulver homestead.

The Order was signed by Francis Gore, Lieutenant-Governor of Upper Canada and granted in 1816 by an order in council a month previous.

The Pulvers acquired their parcel largely from inheritance as the grandmother and grandfather of Herbert Pulver, a Mr. and Mrs. Cunningham, acquired the one portion by means of a mortgage taken on the Rush property. Neither John Rush nor his wife Elizabeth Rush, were able to read or write hence their mark on legal documents, but their daughter, Margaret, who married William Albert Grey, had acquired enough education to at least write her name. A small parcel of an acre or less was purchased from Elizabeth Rush, widow of John Rush, and her daughter, by David Pulver in 1872. David Pulver willed the farm to his son Herbert, the latter to take possession on the attainment of his twenty-first birthday. The elder Pulver, however, passed on when his son was but fifteen years old, so after his death the chattels were disposed of and the farm was worked by a cousin until the owner should become of age, so, when the young couple were ready to start their life work, the job was undertaken with a little money and a grim determination to succeed.

As a start the young farmer bought two Jersey cows across the bay from a man by the name of Brown and this pair along with a cow and a calf which the bride had received from her father, was the herd planned for the first year's operations.

"But", as Mr. Pulver expressed in his story to me, "we had bad luck with our cows. I turned them out in the orchard, a place where the grass had been cut early or perhaps not at all the summer before and there was plenty of what I thought was good pasture. Not more than a week after I went to the barn one morning and one of the Jerseys was dead. That was quite a blow but not as much as the one which followed. The next week my wife's cow also took sick. There were no phones and of course no cars in those days, so I drove to Belleville to get Dr. Purvis who was the practising veterinary at that time in the town. He arrived as soon as possible and did what he could for the cow, but his best wasn't quite good enough and that cow died too.

That was the beginning of the farming operations of young Mr. and Mrs. Pulver. To this union were born three sons, Melvin in 1902, Arza in 1907 and Winston in 1913. In 1912, with the foresight that had always been characteristic of them, a second farm was purchased on the Gore from the estate of the late Fred Redner, and on his marriage to Annie Price the eldest son, Melvin, assumed ownership of the original Pulver property. Today, he is Deputy-Reeve of the township of Ameliasburgh and follows the footsteps of his father for good farming and good management. This year saw a further diversification when his son Morris and young wife took over the homestead and Mr. and Mrs. Melvin Pulver moved to another farm on the same road which had been acquired a few years previous.

The second son, Arza, passed on in 1946. He, too, had a farm of his own — two farms distant from ours and he and I were buddies. We worked and played together. We drew in hay, we drew peas, cut wood and did perhaps a thousand other jobs and our recreation was mostly going fishing.

The third son, Winston, now operates the farm on which father and son reside and those two original milking cows have been increased to sixteen and their home and farm today may be looked upon as up-to-date in every way .

Lorne Brickman's Canning Factory.
8,800 pounds of jam were shipped from here overseas during World War I.

The Brickmans

If you chanced to meet Lorne Brickman at any kind of a function you would take him to be a man in his middle sixties, find him to be a good conversationalist and also that he was well versed in the history of both his community and the local church with which he has been connected since its construction.

The Brickman name can be linked with the earliest history of the Township of Ameliasburgh because in the middle of the eighteenth century the earliest settler by that name came directly from Holland and was granted two hundred acres from the crown consisting of the two farms still in the Brickman name, the one belonging to Lorne Brickman on the Gore and the other directly north to the Bay of Quinte owned by the widow of the late Elijah Brickman. When the farms were separated in the time of the son of the first settler the latter parcel of land retained the crown deed but neither farm has ever been owned by any one of any other name.

LUDWIG BRICKMAN brought his family with him from Holland and like most other early pioneers had to clear land to erect his log house and barn. Those were not built on the site of the present buildings, as at that time no roads existed, but were situated approximately three-eighths of a mile due north on a limestone ridge which commences on the northwest corner of our own farm running westward and finally widening out to the entire width of the township.

A story is told of Ludwig, of his liking for horses — and also liquor. He was an extremely kind man to all the farm animals and was never known to drive his horses off a walk, except on one occasion. He always kept a string of bells around their necks and whenever his few neighbours heard their jingle they shook their heads and said to themselves or remarked to each other, "Ludwig has had a drink today".

RYNARD carried on in his father's footsteps and established a lime kiln and built up a considerable business. He had four sons who, when the kiln was built of the hardest hardheads they could find, gathered limestones all across the ridge and sold the finished product for twenty-five cents a bushel to provide spending money for themselves. The present owner dismantled the old kiln not so many years previously and told me that some of the stones were sufficiently large that a team of horses had to be used to draw them to a fence corner.

Their source of water was a well near the old buildings and in the summer when the water level was lowest these hardy old pioneers would have to go down a ladder and dip the water from a small basin in the bottom of the well, but no matter how much they dipped from that small basin the level of the water never went any lower.

The first house on the present location was built by Rynard shortly after the township was surveyed something over a century and a half ago. When the first roads were established a new log house was built on the site of their present one but as an improvement to the house on the hill this one boasted a cellar, not much more than a hole in the ground, but it served as a place to store fruits and vegetables. Fruit was not too plentiful, especially in the way of apples, but an orchard had been set out near the old buildings on the hill as soon as the land could be cleared sufficiently. It was the first orchard in the community and though it contained only common fruit the boys used to like to crawl through the fence and fill their pockets. William Cronk, once a neighbour, but afterward settling in Sophiasburgh, was one of the boys who knew where the holes in the fence were and made the remark "They tasted good but oh boy! they were sour".

While still a boy Lorne, the present owner, helped his father cut the trees, some of which attained a diameter of two feet, burned the brush and in later years the stumps rotted permitting the field to be tilled.

One of the outstanding qualities of the second log house was its huge fireplace which could accommodate several logs at one time. A horse was usually used to draw the backlog right into the kitchen and once that was put in place several small ones could be put in front. The backlog under ordinary circumstances lasted three or four days.

Rynard's son Lewis followed him as owner of the property

and was a very righteous man who worked hard but never on Sunday. In his time the land to the north of the road was a dense maple bush and during the sugar season this job held priority over all else. He would boil sap from Monday morning till Saturday night almost continuously, but when the stroke of twelve came all operations ceased, but just as surely when the hour of twelve rolled around on Sunday night the Brickmans resumed their work in the sugarbush. They boiled it all in a potash kettle and for summer use had a hogshead of syrup which was around eighty gallons and a thousand pounds of sugar. This was the only sweet the ladies knew in those days and consequently was used for all culinary purposes. A hurricane, however, ripped through the district and one by one those noble maples bowed their heads and that storm wrote finis to the maple sugar industry on the Brickman farm.

The second house had been built some time in the middle of the nineteenth century while the next house is now used as a canning factory by the Brickmans. It was built by a local carpenter, Daniel DeLong, whose son Milton still lives in Belleville. Lewis Brickman decided that the time had arrived when he should be an inhabitant of something more up to date than the old log house so as a result of that desire, he set out to construct a building of entirely new design.

The timber for the new house was entirely hand hewn and the lumber sawed at a mill which was run by water power and situated up the creek or marsh as most of us know it today. A large dam had been constructed some forty rods west of the road approaching the John Black poultry farm from the north. In its heyday that mill did all the custom work for miles around but one spring an unusually large freshet caused an ice jam to take out the dam and it was never rebuilt as the farmers upstream had suffered too much damage from flooded land. All the remains of the old mill and dam have vanished years ago. There were few if any shingle mills in those days and the shingles were all hand made from virgin pine and were perhaps three times as thick as the ones we see at the present time. They were of such good material and workmanship that they made a satisfactory covering for the roof for well over a hundred years. The floors were of inch and a half pine and all the moulding was hand planed.

In 1936 the persent owner tore up this floor to make room for a new boiler for his factory and underneath, on one of the beams, he discovered an old bottle of whiskey which had been removed from circulation for at least a couple of generations. Lorne Brickman, unlike his forefather Ludwig, had no taste for alcoholic beverages and what is more entertained no desire to further anyone elses along that line so the spirits were combined with camphor and placed on the pantry shelf for future medicinal use as an alleviative for headaches and muscular pains.

LEWIS' son RYNARD, named after his grandfather, was the fourth generation to till the soil and tread the paths of his forefathers and it is in no small way due to the progressiveness and ingenuity of this gentleman that the Brickman farm has taken on its present day appearance. He built the barn during the latter part of the last century and as the farm had been largely depleted of its original woodlot the lumber was purchased at three dollars per thousand for siding and teamed across the ice from Trenton. The material for rafters was secured from John Harvey Brown on the second concession of our township near what is now Highway No. 33. They had a regular old-fashioned barn raising that summer and tables were set outside the old house in June 1898, when one hundred men and thirty women sat down to supper. One of the contributions made by Mrs. Brickman senior toward the meal was sixteen pans of chicken pie made in the old-fashioned milk pans which were so much in evidence in those days.

During the first few years of the new century Rynard was also instrumental in constructing their house but only enjoyed its comforts four years after its construction when he passed from this life leaving the estate to his son Lorne.

Mr. and Mrs. Lorne Brickman have long been connected with Victoria Church, he as superintendent of the Sunday School for forty years and recording steward of the circuit of Rednersville for more than twenty-five years as well as holding many other positions in connection with church work. Mrs. Brickman has been a member of the choir, organist, president of the missionary society and in addition doing a kindly deed in any time of need. He served as president of Quinte factory for five years and boarded as high as one hundred and sixty-seven cheese in one week. He was also president of the amalgamated factories of Mountain View and Highland for three years and headed Belleville district with the highest number of cheese on the board .

During the depression years the sale of canned vegetables

and fruits was curtailed to a greater extent than was good for either the producer or consumer. It was in one of these years that the canning factories refused point blank to take delivery of tomatoes. He had contracts with two separate factories but this failed to be any advantage so he rented a home canning outfit from King and Rankin in Belleville and started in the canning business. His rent cost forty dollars and they, he and his family, canned four hundred cases which he sold the following spring to National Grocers at a small profit. The next year he bought an outfit and canned corn, tomatoes and beans. Then gradually other lines were added to include asparagus, tomato juice and chicken. During their experience in custom work the family have canned many different lines of meat including venison and rabbit.

The factory was used for jam making for the Red Cross during World War II and neighbouring women gave their time to assist and a special permit was obtained from that organization for the sugar used. Mrs. McLean of Rednersville weighed all fruit and sugar and 8,800 pounds of jam were canned and shipped overseas.

Lorne Brickman and Emma Ainsworth were married at Burrs by Rev. Bamforth and have celebrated their fifty-second wedding anniversary. They have one daughter, Audra.

Thus another saga has been written of our hardy pioneers who, with courage and faith of all those who seek their fortune in new and little known lands, have endured untold hardships but through those hardships have paved the way for their descendants, of whom we form a part, to live in that land and be classed among the most privileged people in the world; privileged to worship in our own way; to feel that our bodies are well and properly nourished; to be able to enjoy the right of free speech and a host of other rights and perhaps of equal importance to be able to thank God that men like Ludwig Brickman chose a land called Canada upon which to bestow their future generations.

Oscar Burley's Reminiscences

Oscar Burley was born in Cressy on December 22, 1862.

The Burleys were of French descent and of the Roman Catholic faith and Oscar's great aunt was a nun and a high official of the old church of that denomination on the Bath road. His grandfather married a Huff and after the marriage forsook that faith and became one of the stalwarts of the old Wesleyan Methodist Church at Cressy and was a prominent official at the time of the building of that edifice on the south shore or lake shore of the point. Everyone attended the Wesleyan Church at that time but in later years a split developed in its ranks — the insurgents being led by the Wright family with the result that an Episcopalian Methodist Church was built on the north or bay side.

Both buildings are still there, but the subject of our story and the Oddfellows bought the Wesleyan Church and it was used for an Oddfellows hall. Then the lodge attendance dwindled almost to the vanishing point so the remaining few members transferred the ownership to the Women's Institute for a hall, so it is now used for all community enterprises and is kept in an excellent state of repair by that organization. The Episcopalian is now used as a United Church on a circuit comprising Waupoos, Bongard and Glenora in addition to Cressy.

The name of Burley is one of the oldest in the section as land still owned by members of the family can boast of a crown deed.

Oscar got his early education in the old wooden school house on the lake side which has long since been dismantled but the two giant elm trees which shaded the school yard in its earliest days are still standing.

At that time there was considerable rivalry between two factions of people of the bayside and the lakeside. It was two miles across the point and the people on the north side wanted the new school to be located on the crossroad between but those on the lakeside emerged victorious and the location was moved approximately half a mile west. The new school is a modern structure and built of brick.

Henry A. Powers, Oscar's uncle, taught in the old school for eighteen years and had an attendance of sixty in the summer and as high as ninety in the winter when they even had to put chairs on the teacher's platform to make room for all. Henry was good in bookkeeping and four of his pupils came all the way from Picton to further their studies in this subject. He had pupils up to twenty-four years of age in the winter time. Boys and girls never went to collegiate then but Oscar came within sixteen marks of getting a third class certificate from public school. "But school is different now", he said, "and nobody goes to public school after passing the entrance".

The old school, like so many others at the time, had a huge box-stove with the woodhouse being at the back of the building. There were three large windows on each side which gave plenty of light and a good sized porch where the children hung their hats and coats and left their dinner pails. They had snowball fights then as well as now and Oscar, who was quite a wrestler could throw many of the bigger boys including Charlie Denike and Alex MacDonald from Picton. "We could not exactly be classed as angels in those days", he said "but on the whole we were a pretty peaceable lot". All those attending school were forbidden to go out on the ice but frequently they would go out so far that they could not be seen from shore. That was much more dangerous than most of the pupils realized so the teacher made a very fast rule that there were to be no excursions of that nature.

The Burley family consisted of three boys and one girl — Oscar, Edward, Harry and Margaret. Edward took a bookkeeping course in Belleville and clerked for a time in Picton after which he bought a farm in Waupoos where he developed lung trouble so he sold the business and went west. He was the provincial auditor for Alberta for fifteen years and continued in that position until his retirement. He and his wife had two sons, Ralph and Arnold. Ralph was a civil and electrical engineer and served on the waterways commission in the State of New York. He died of an attack of fever and his only son was killed in an accident two years back on the farm at Cressy. Arnold is a lawyer in Edmonton.

Harry, at the ripe old age of eighty-seven is still on the homestead and has two sons — Gerald is public relations officer for the Bell Telephone Company in Toronto and Howard is still on the farm. His sister, Margaret was bookkeeper for Canadian Canners for many years.

Oscar bought his grandfather's farm when he was twenty-seven years of age — soon after he was married to Carrie Hurlbut sixty-six years ago on September 18. His grandfather had passed on and he rented the farm from his grandmother but before he could take possession she too passed away so he found himself immediate owner of a hundred and fifty-acre farm.

Oscar and his wife spent five years on the farm and he was just a little poorer, he thought, at the end of that time than he was when he started. That year the McKinley tariff came into effect and dealt a death blow to the barley market. His father had thirteen hundred bushels and got it away before the tariff became law but Oscar still had eight hundred bushels on hand. After such a discouraging blow he sold the farm to Levi Pearce, and George Anderson, a veteran of the second world war, is the present occupant and owner.

After selling the farm Oscar moved into Picton and started in the machinery business with a Peter Hamilton agency and sold many small lines including horse forks which he usually installed himself even though it was not regarded as a safe business. From the Peter Hamilton line he changed to Frost and Wood. Binders by that time had largely replaced the old-fashioned reapers and milking machines were beginning to come through to take the drudgery out of milking cows. There had been no previous Frost and Wood agency in Picton up to this time and tractors were also beginning to come in to make shorter work hours for the farmer. He had several contracts to supply all the machinery needed to start a farm. For several years from 1905 he had his showroom where the *Gazette* office now is and had E. T. Plews as a partner. The latter served for years as a director of the Bay of Quinte Fire Insurance Company. He sold out the machinery business to Charlton Metcalfe and his father and travelled for four years as block man for the Frost and Wood Company with a territory extending from Cobourg to Napanee and including Prince Edward County.

One day there appeared an advertisement in the local paper that the Chevrolet was coming to Picton and that an agency would be opened up in due time to serve the town and surrounding district. A DeLaval traveller, who dropped in for a chat with Oscar, thought it looked like a good proposition with a promising future. Chevrolets, new cars on the market at the time, were to be made in Toronto but before any agencies were let the McLaughlins bought out the Chevrolet business and started to manufacture their cars in Oshawa. That meant that the agencies already held by the men selling that make of buggies would have preference in the newly allotted contracts appointing dealers all across Canada. Dave Lambert sold McLaughlin buggies in Picton and was, by virtue of that position, in line for the car agency to be given out by that company. On the appointed day Oscar made known his wishes and the man who had the letting of the contract asked him if he were the Burley who had been with the Frost and Wood. He had heard very good reports of him, he said, as he had also been connected with the company and he was very sorry that it was impossible for him to go beyond his orders but said that Mr. Lambert was to be given first opportunity. "But", he added, "You be here tomorrow at one o'clock and if he does not come at that time the agency will be yours."

The next day at one-thirty Oscar Burley left McLaughlin Carriage Company in Oshawa with a contract in his pocket — the first for Chevrolet cars in the County of Prince Edward. Mr. Lambert turned up at two o'clock but after giving him the benefit of half an hour he was half an hour too late.

"Those were the days when it was fun to sell cars as nobody had one and every family was a potential customer", he told me but he also reminded me that in those days one could buy a new car for six or seven hundred dollars and everybody seemed to have more money than they have today.

The first cars he got in stock only had three doors, two front and one right rear and canvas tops. However the model was changed after that and the new ones had the fourth door. The first cars were driven down from Oshawa and as neither one of the partners in the business could drive a car at that time they engaged Ray Clapp, the local veterinarian, to go up and bring them down to their sales room. The first sale they made was to Rae Fox on the high shore road.

George Johnson had the Ford agency at the time and that was the only competition when they started business. "The Chev. had a little more power than the old Model T Ford but it wouldn't climb much of a hill without putting it in second", he said. Frank Boulter and George Farrington had the first cars in Picton but they were chain driven and were painfully slow and very noisy. It would take an hour and a half to go to Milford and back and they had hard tires which made them ride pretty rough.

"They were very crude outfits alongside the high-powered cars of today," he remarked, "but probably safer too".

One of his favourite stories was about the time he sold a new car to Claude Kotchapaw. Oscar was out in the morning and made a call on that gentleman and during the course of his travels sold one to Morris Huff. On the way home he made a second sale and after dinner he and his partner, Charlie Metcalfe, arrived back at the Kotchapaw farm just after George Johnson drove in with a Ford. They talked a few minutes and Oscar said "We came here to sell a car so let's get at it". Claude went for a ride in the Ford and the competitors, not to be outdone, invited Mrs. Kotchapaw to ride in the Chev. After Claude came back he expressed his regrets to Charlie and Oscar and told them he had made up his mind to

D. K. Redner in his 1917 Model-T Ford

buy a Ford. But he had not reckoned on the good judgement of his wife. "You are not going to buy any until you have had a ride in this Chev.", she told her husband. Charlie and Oscar went down to Joe Roblin's for supper and, as Claude and Joe were friends, the latter sent up word that if Claude would buy a Chev. he would too. As a result the partners got the two men together and wrote up the orders by the lights of their demonstrator which was the sixth Chevrolet sold in Canada. That made four sales in one day and another afternoon they sold three in one man's barnyard. "The first winter", he said "we filled John Hubbs' canning factory, Crystal Palace at the fair grounds and all the other space we could get with new cars and sold them all. The only trade-in was an occasional buggy but there was a considerable demand for good buggies so these were readily turned over".

They had the Chevrolet agency for five years and then Oscar sold Willys, Nash and Dodge and had his garage opposite Jones' grocery where Roblin Motor Sales is at present. He had the first clear vision pump in town for gasoline and sold Imperial products. He had the best gasoline business in Picton and was open every night until ten o'clock and only with difficulty did he get closed by midnight on Saturday night.

When asked to what did he attribute his longevity he replied "Hard work. I have always been active and accustomed to being busy. The only sickness I ever had was touches of chronic appendicitis and now at ninety-two I think I have outgrown it".

Fair Grounds, Picton, Ont. (Courtesy: Vic Lord, Picton.)

The Anderson Family

William Anderson, born in Ireland, and his descendants were destined to play an important part in the government of Upper Canada as well as the Township of Ameliasburgh where they eventually settled. The senior Anderson was born on the 28th day of May 1786 in the County of Monoghan in the northern part of what is now Eire.

WILLIAM ANDERSON emigrated with his parents to New York State at the early age of six years and came to Canada about the year 1800 and was admitted a member of the Free and Accepted Masons at Ernesttown on the 27th of March 1806. He remained a member of that order until the time of his death in June 1869 and had the distinction of being a Mason for the extremely long period of sixty-three years. His descendants also followed his example in this respect and many have been affiliated with the order since that time.

On the first of July 1810 he married Mary Way and they settled near Mountain View and worked together for fifty-seven years. He did duty in the war with the United States in 1812 and afterwards held a commission in the militia. He joined the Methodist Church in 1824 and retained a commission with the church until he died. He was also a commissioner in the court of Request for several years. His wife predeceased him but both lived to see their large family grow up and respectably settled. The family consisted of five sons, William, John, Levi, George and James. William was the politician of the family and was member of parliament at the time when members sat for both the Provincial House and the House of Upper Canada. He sat for the term of parliament previous to 1863 but in that year was defeated in the general election by Lt.-Col. Walter Ross who in turn defeated Jas. S. McCuaig on three separate occasions. He was twice married, taking Arvilla Potts for his first wife and Elizabeth Giles for the second. His first family consisted of three boys, George, Alex and Willoughby, while the second was two girls, Letta who became Mrs. McCauley and Libby, who married a man by the name of

Steele. His obituary appeared in the Picton paper of December 24th, 1897 and reads as follows:

> About midnight last night, Mr. William Anderson, ex-M.P.P., was found dead on the road leading from the Union Church, Ameliasburgh, to his home. Mr. Anderson had been in Belleville yesterday and returned to his home in the afternoon and went to a tea meeting in the Union Church about one mile from his home. He left the meeting about half past nine and about twelve was found dead on the road only a few rods from the church. Heart failure was supposed to have been the cause of his death. Mr. Anderson had been a life-long Conservative and for nearly forty years had been prominent in this county in federal and municipal politics. In 1861 he was first elected representative of Prince Edward County to the old parliament of Canada, defeating Dr. Dorland. In the general election of 1864 he was again candidate but this time was defeated by Mr. Walter Ross. After confederation Mr. Greely was the first representative from Prince Edward to the Provincial Parliament. Before his time expired the shrievalty of this county became vacant by the death of Sheriff McDonald and Mr. Greely was appointed sheriff, thus vacating his seat. In the election which followed to fill the vacancy Mr. Anderson was the Conservative candidate defeating Mr. Pamelius Sprague. He was reeve of the township for several years consecutively, Warden of the County of Prince Edward for one year and was a prominent patron and president of the Prince Edward Association since its organization in 1893. He was a member of the Methodist Church and was a local preacher.

William's sons, George, Alex and Willoughby, all followed the call of the soil but George sold out and moved to Toronto while Alex and Willoughby purchased farms on the front road, the former from J. W. Way and the latter from R. B. Morden — a property which had been in the Morden name since it had been granted from the Crown. Alex never aspired to political office but the quality was passed on to Willoughby who was on two occasions assessor for the township and also held the office of collector. He was for years a member of the township council serving as councillor, deputy-reeve and reeve and in addition occupied the warden's chair for a term.

In my years of living in the township I have always wondered why no crossroad ever existed between Rednersville and Rossmore between the first and second concessions, but like many other items of historical interest which I have collected, the answer to this question was given to me by Jerald Anderson. He is Willoughby's only son and told of a travelled road which ran back Mrs. Harry Anderson's lane across the back end of their own place and thence across a floating bridge, the road joining what is now Highway No. 14 on the turn just north of the farm occupied by George Jackson. In the years gone by a cheese factory was situated on the bay shore on the place owned by Ernest Teney and with it a grain warehouse where farmers on the lower front drew their grain (mostly barley) to ship to the United States for making beer. It was an every day occurrence for people from the second concession or anyone south of the marsh to use this road, especially during the busy season to draw their grain to the Anderson shore.

A story is told of Willoughby who, when serving as collector, was using the floating bridge to return home one dark night with the receipts of the day's collections. The back end of both the Anderson properties was heavily wooded and as he neared this part of the homeward journey he saw a light along the side of the road. Fearing any consequences which might follow, he turned the horse around, retraced his steps and spent the night on the south shore and resumed the homeward journey in daylight.

* * *

WILLOUGHBY married Annie White for his first wife and a daughter, Muriel, was born to the union. He then married Edna Burr who passed on in 1950 leaving one son, Jerald who followed his father's footsteps and was a member of both township and county councils. He married Gladys Wells in 1932 and they have two daughters, Margaret and Marilyn. He operates a hundred acre farm and today may be counted as one of the most prosperous farmers on the front road.

ALEX married Blanche Babbit and two children graced this household, Roy and Clara. Roy sold his farm to Brigadier Genet but has recently purchased the summer home of A. E. Purdy on the front road. They have no children.

GEORGE'S family and descendants have all moved to distant fields. He married Sarah Giles.

Perhaps the outstanding achievement of James was the building of the ferry *Mary Ethel.* Undoubtedly Captain James Anderson was also a very prominent figure in the community — not politically, but commercially, because during his years of operating the ferry he carried notable visitors to the county as well as the ordinary traffic with horses and vehicles or the ordinary man on foot. His wife was Theodicia Brickman and their children were Harry, Edward, Fred and Mrs. Stanley Wellbanks. Harry's farm is still carried on by his widow on the front road. They had one daughter who married Sherman Babbit.

JOHN married Mary Roblin and they had eleven children including Ridley and Howard which are perhaps the best known in Ameliasburgh.

LEVI married Mary Farley for his first wife and later Debbie Jones. They had seven children including Alf., Jay and James R. who is the father of John, Ben and Lily.

This is perhaps the most complete record of the older settlers of any one family that I have attempted to trace. The five sons of William Anderson had a combined total of thirty-three children in their families yet today there are no male heirs to carry on the name which has played such an important part in the development of the township of Ameliasburgh and the county as a whole. Time creates many changes in a community and families who are prominent in one generation are lost to the observation of the ordinary citizen of the next. The Staffords, the Mordens, the Glenns, the Petersons and many others have figured largely in the history of our twonship and yet today those names have been or will shortly be erased from the citizenry of their former communities.

Regrettable as it may seem the next generation will see the Andersons coming into the same classification and their name will be no more in the lists of township residents. It may be just another case of history repeating itself but we might do with a little less repetition in such instances where nature makes it necessary to observe the gradual elimination of family names who have played such prominent parts in the development of our small part of the world.

Herb Love's Reminiscences

The Love family originally came from Ireland but unlike many others of our original settlers did not enter the country from the United States but emigrated directly from the mother country to Black Creek. Samuel, Herb's grandfather, was the original settler and came to this country as a young man. He had seven sons one of whom stayed on the farm and another lived in Picton. The farm at Black Creek is now owned by people by the name of Church or rather the widow of the family as Mr. Church passed on some time ago.

JAMES LOVE settled in Picton where he became a contractor and operated a planing mill in connection with his business. Among the houses he built was one on Queen Street for his son Herb after the latter's marriage to Margaret Argue in Cobourg, August 23rd, 1898.

HERB LOVE received his early education in Picton public and high schools and started as a telegraph messenger boy with a a local firm of John A. Rawson of Great Northwestern Telegraph Co. who was the first railway agent in Picton and in addition had a brokerage office and sold stocks and bonds and changed money.

The government would not grant a charter to the original railway so it had to be built entirely by private capital and was known as the Prince Edward Railway serving the entire countryside around Picton and the section from Picton to Trenton. The two locomotives to first see service on the road were named *The Picton* and *The Trenton*, the latter being considerably larger and consequently able to haul a much larger load than the *Picton*. Both were equipped with wood burning engines as it was considered too costly a proposition to burn coal when wood was so cheap.

Alexander Manning, a broker in Toronto, had put up sufficient money to purchase a right-of-way for the road sometime about the middle seventies, and shares were sold to many local people to assist with its building. John Haney of Toronto, was entrusted with the job of superintendent of construction and Chas. Bokus was vice-president. William Marrow was its first secretary and treasurer and his son, also William, was the first station agent at Consecon. The head office was for a time in Trenton but the road ran into financial difficulties and was put on the auction block and was purchased by McMullen brothers for a man by the name of Ritchie in Akron, Ohio. The McMullen brothers took over the management of the road and the locomotives which were put into service at this time carried the name of all the brothers but this system was soon changed and each engine was given a number — a system that has been carried down through the years and today every engine is identified by its number.

After the disposal of the road to the Ritchie and McMullen interests it was decided to extend the line to Coe Hill as iron ore had been found in that district and it was expected that years of business would ensue from its building. To accomplish this extension would mean that additional capital would have to be secured, so a body of Cleveland men was approached by Mr. Ritchie, the proposition put before them and upon investigation they put up sufficient capital to finish the road which up to this time had been controlled entirely by S. J. Ritchie and the McMullens. Mr. Ritchie favoured the building of a smelter in Trenton but the Cleveland interests would have none of this idea as they wanted the ore to be brought to their own city before smelting.

The McMullens were invested with powers to control and extend the road and this was done — on both ends. The Picton end ran only to the edge of the town not far from where the cold storage plant is at present and was extended as far as the station. Some years after it was extended to its present limits. George W. McMullen became president after its re-organization, J. B. McMullen became vice-president, D. S. came down from Chatham to superintend the northern end of the construction; D. V. was a very small man and he handled the finances of the company while H. C. was agent at Picton. Two years later Howard McMullen was recalled from that office and Herb Love who had become operator was appointed in his place and retained the position for over fifty years.

One of the outstanding developments of the road in as much as Prince Edward was concerned was the building of the docks at Weller's Bay. After the failure of the railway owners to agree on the Trenton smelter a quarter of a million dollars was spent to provide a roundhouse and docks on the south side of Weller's Bay from where ore was shipped for a year on a boat operated by Captain VanDusen who sailed continuously between that place and Cleveland. After Mr. Ritchie and the McMullens secured control of the road the head office was moved to Picton from Trenton for a couple of years until the new station was built at the latter place. The large desk now in use at the baggage room in the local station was the one used by the McMullens in their original Trenton office. After the line was built to Coe Hill it became known as the Central Ontario Railway and was eventually extended to Bancroft.

After a year's operation of the whole line the Ritchie interests and the Cleveland financiers battled for its control and after it had swung back and forth several times like the pendulum on a grand-father clock in the front hall, the whole system was disposed of to the Grand Trunk. By the time the latter made the purchase the best of the known ore had been removed from the north country and the roundhouse was moved to Trenton while the dock where so much activity had taken place fell into disuse. The water level rose in the lake and the wharf was submerged for decades but one year not far back it went down sufficiently to allow partial dismantling and plank from the dock was sold to any interested parties one of whom was Lee Rowe who secured enough to cover the stalls in his horse stable.

Herb Love was the proudest man in Picton the morning he started to work in the new station. The railway purchased the land between that building and front street and for many years it was a well cared for lawn. There was a real passenger service in those days as cars and trucks were only coming into being. The station agent was usually on the job at eight in the morning and worked until six and nine o'clock on Saturday night but for two years extra service was given which left at six in the morning, so this necessitated his being there to sell tickets for that train. During this period there were three passenger trains daily each way, the second arriving at eight-thirty a.m. and leaving at nine while the afternoon train came in at one-thirty and left about two hours later. The early morning train arrived back in town late that night. The early and late train was only on for about two years but the other two were still on when Herb retired twenty years ago. Billy Nettleton was express agent for nearly fifty years and saw all kinds of goods go out and come in.

In the earlier days coal was mostly brought in by water but after the railway had been in operation for some time much of it was brought by that method although the Hepburn Company owned a fleet of boats.

Herb remembers the town when you could get in up to your ankles in the mud on main street in the early spring and all the sidewalks on the main street were made of wood. Frasers was one of the firms doing business in those early days and both papers were as much in evidence as they are today. The post office was in the building where the telephone office is now and he has seen the coming of the armouries and the theatre as well as the new post office.

ANDREW IRVING and JOHN DOWNS were among the town's influential citizens and had not only a contracting business with offices where Hepburn's coal shed is now but also a saw mill and did all kinds of custom work. The yard was usually filled with logs which came from all around the countryside. A man by the name of Harper ran a sash and door factory in the west end of town and made all kinds of mouldings as well as sash and doors.

The incoming freight was mostly goods for the shops and canning factories in town while the freight shipped out was largely canned goods and farm produce including livestock.

A. C. Miller and Company, whose factory is now but an old building down back of the theatre, was one of the early shippers of canned goods. The Old Homestead factory was built by Amos Baker who was backed financially by Richardson Bros., grain merchants of Kingston. At the time of its building it was looked upon as one of the finest factories in Canada and was entirely of concrete construction. All their goods were shipped by rail and ownership in the meantime has passed to Canadian Canners.

All the cattle and hogs were shipped by rail and from eight to twenty cars in the busiest part of the season left Picton weekly for either packing houses or to be used for dairy purposes.

The town had two seed houses; the Cleveland seed house down on the high shore road was run by O. L. Daily but the building across the road from the hospital has long since been torn down. Daily acted as agent for a St. Vincent firm in New York State but eventually discontinued business. The other was run by the John H. Allen seed company also of St. Vincent. H. T. Hopkins was manager and this business was backed by a man by the name of Parmalee who had made a fortune out of pills over in New York State. This business was later purchased by Hogg and Lytle who shipped seed peas and clover seeds to all parts of Canada and the United States.

Main Street, East, Picton, Ont. (Courtesy: Vic Lord, Picton.)

The Moy Family

On Christmas Day 1901, Marcus Moy, son of Mr. and Mrs. Walter Moy of Mountain View, was united in the holy bonds of matrimony to Emma Way, daughter of John F. Way and Janey Blanchard of Centre neighbourhood. Amid best wishes the newly-weds left for West Lake on their honeymoon. The night was clear and frosty and it was much father to West Lake with a horse and cutter than with a high-powered automobile, but they arrived in due time and perhaps spent as happy a honeymoon as anyone at the present time.

The Moys were of English descent, Mr. Moy Sr. having migrated from near Yarmouth in the County of Norfolk on England's east coast. He had spent some years as a fisherman, being employed by a local company and on one occasion a storm ripped the masts from the ship and she drifted helplessly for four days when the crew was picked up by another boat. About 1875 he quite suddenly came to a decision to quit the fishing business and come to Canada, so almost immediately began to carry out his resolution and the end of the year found him in a new world.

The groom of 1901 first saw the light of day in a little log house situated perhaps the width of a hundred acres directly east of Mountain View cheese factory. At the age of four the family moved to Gilead but remained there only a year as the Moys were devoutly religious people and found it too far to go to church. Moving back to their old community they spent the next twelve years on a farm then owned by S. S. Potter and now occupied by James Robinson. Little Marcus spent his first day at school in Gilead and on the way home two or three of the bigger boys took his older brother down and told the little lad they had killed him. That so frightened Marcus that never again could he be persuaded to go to school in Gilead. The next year, however, he started to school at Mountain View and, though he had a long way to go, always walked because his father did not own a horse. The whole family walked to Mountain View to attend church on Sunday and all the way to Roblin's Mills to Quarterly Meeting four times a year.

At that time Mr. Potter ran a canning factory in the building, now occupied by Stanley Barber as a garage, and canned asparagus, peas, corn and tomatoes.

One of the outstanding differences between the canning industry of those days and today was the problem of cans. The large can companies had either not come into being or had not catered to the small factory so in conjunction with his canning business Mr. Potter ran a tin smith's shop. In a room over the factory he employed two workmen during the entire packing season and these two men made all the cans from sheets of tin about three feet square, a size which could be used to the best advantage for making the finished product. On only one occasion did he suffer any loss from his pack and that was one year's pea crop which, due to poor workmanship in the cans or some other unknown condition, bulged after the pack and many of them exploded.

Mrs. Moy for many years, worked in Mr. Potter's canning factory and top wages by the hourly rate was five cents per hour. They usually worked ten hours a day and in fine weather all the women walked to work — some as far as two miles, but on rainy days the factory owner picked them up with a covered wagon drawn by one horse.

After twelve years of service to Mr. Potter the Moys moved to Massassaga on the farm where Wesley Way now lives and worked that place for one year, returning at the end of that time to the farm they had left the year before, this time purchasing it from the man they had worked for so long.

Marcus lived and worked with his father for five years and then came the eventful day of December 25th, 1901, when he took as his life partner Emma Way, who by a curious turn of events, resided in the same house now occupied by their only son, Morley and his wife, approximately a quarter mile from the Moy farm.

After their marriage the young couple lived in the house across the road from the Potter business — the house now used as a domicile by J. D. Keeble — and Marcus worked one more year with his father after which he returned to the employ of Mr. Potter where he stayed until February 1905 when he and his brother-in-law, James Halliday, rented a farm from James Elliott — the farm where the Moys now reside. The partnership was dissolved three years later when the Hallidays returned to buy a farm which they had previously rented from Dr. Sprague in Belleville and which in the meantime had been purchased by Ernest Wallbridge. The Hallidays still live on the farm.

James Peck, born 1803

The Peck Family and Albury

Next to the Holy Bible, Noah Webster wrote or compiled the most important book in the world — the dictionary — with its almost innumerable explanations of the meanings of words.

The word romance is listed through the modern English period with several meanings but I shall single out one: "A tendency of mind toward the wonderful and mysterious". The use of the word today is usually looked upon as the attraction of one sex to the other and a situation of that nature developed around the middle of the eighteenth century in the state of New Jersey when James and Elizabeth Peck fell in love. They had been born at the same place — at Schraalenburg in the Township of Herrington in Bergen County, New Jersey. He was born on May 4th, 1759, while the date of Elizabeth's birth was six years later on April 10, 1765.

There was apparently some parental objection to the eventual marriage of the young couple due probably to the evident fact that there may have been some relationship between them but such a situation had no deterrent effect on the enthusiasm of the young people because at the tender age of twenty years Elizabeth set out with James for parts unknown. The latter's father owned and operated the ferry across the Hudson River from the State of New Jersey to Manhattan Island or what is now Jersey City to New York City and both families were apparently well-to-do but Elizabeth had what money they possessed as they left the parental roof.

Their journey proved to be an extended one and their wordly possessions were decidedly few, including as a mode of conveyance a blind mare and some kind of a carriage. The mare was accompanied by her colt. How long the journey took we are not told but it finally ended in Granville, Nova Scotia on the shore of the Annapolis basin. Here two of their ten children were born. Wellempy on December 5th, 1785 and a second son, Samuel two years later on September 8th, 1787.

Little at the time of their departure did they realize that a century and a half later they would be grandfather and grandmother to a prosperous and enterprising community of which at that time they had never even heard.

Some time after the birth of their second child they returned to New York City to settle the estate of James' father and they remained there for several years during which time the ferry business was disposed of and a third child, this time a daughter, Margaret, was born. Her birth place is listed as New York City on March 16th, 1792.

Their loyalty to the Crown may have prompted their return to Canada or it may have been their yearning for further adventure as they chose Big Island for their new home and remained here while two more of their children were born, Rachel October 6th, 1796, and Sarah September 29th, 1798. Not long after that, about September 1800, a new colony was preparing to settle on the south shore of the Bay of Quinte and the Pecks once more moved to a new home which in later years became Albury. This must have been the long hoped for promised land because here they remained. After their arrival here five more children were born, Mary in 1800, James in 1803, John in 1804, Elizabeth in 1806 and Catharine in 1811.

So many later residents have been descended from this noble couple that a large percentage of the people on the front road today as well as the back concessions trace their ancestry to James and Elizabeth Peck. I cannot lay claim to be counted among those but feel justified along with so many others in referring to them as grandfather and grandmother Peck. She passed on in 1825 at the age of sixty and was one of the first if not the first to be laid to rest in the acre of land donated by her for a church, school house and burying ground. James Peck died eleven years later in 1836 and his remains were placed beside those of his wife and companion in adventure in the little cemetery which by this time had become established as the resting place for the departed ones of the community.

Space will not permit me to follow the complete lineage of the family but to demonstrate the large numbers of their descendants I mention part of their family's marriages — those who had a particular bearing on the future population of Ameliasburgh township:

Samuel married Letty Bonter, 1808. Died 1866.

Margaret (born in New York) married Rynard Brickman,

grandfather of Lorne, in June, 1811. (No record of her death.)

Rachel married Joseph Allison in 1818. Died 1828.
Mary married John Weese in 1821. Died 1862.
James married Anna Weese 1826. Died 1882.
John married Catharine Cole 1827. Died 1864.
Catharine married Chas. Robert Bonter 1826. Died 1872.

The first Peck settlement was in Albury community just west of the house which in years within most of our memories was occupied by the late Pem. Peck and family across the road from the church. The house was built on land still under the Peck name but on the farm to the west of the one occupied by Pem. and now owned by Miss Hattie who spent many years in the nursing profession. To this original log dwelling on lot ninety-one a frame wood-shed was added some time afterward and this latter section was moved years later to form part of the house occupied by Pem. The original grant to the Pecks from the crown was something over a hundred acres and the deed was in grandmother Peck's name. That explains why full credit must be given to her for the donation of the land for the church, school house and burying gound which at one time were all part of one property. She owned the farm where Hattie resides, the place to the east where Pem. lived and afterward purchased the farm still to the east of that where Will lives at the present time.

JAMES HENRY, the seventh child of the original settlers, stayed on the old place and farmed and fished. He also had a shoe shop upstairs in the house and made shoes for all his own family and besides did a small amount of custom work for the neighbours. All sewing was done by hand and the leather fastened in an old wooden clamp such as was in common use in those times. The heels were fastened with wooden shoe pegs made of hard maple and it was an almost unknown fact that nails could be used for that same purpose.

His family consisted of nine children, the eighth of whom was John Greer, father of Harry. The family also included Francis, Samuel, William and Myron Wesley.

JOHN, the youngest son of the original settlers also farmed and in later years attended market with his son Henry. John had two sons, Stephen and Henry, and three daughters one of whom,

Betsy by name, married Thomas Dempsey, Herb's father. Henry had two sons, Stephen who died childless and Marshal who lives in Deseronto.

SAMUEL, the next oldest of James Henry's sons became a lawyer and went to Minden in Haliburton where he was elected Liberal member of Parliament (contrary to the traditional Peck policies) and was eventually elevated to the judgeship of Victoria county. He afterward moved to the United States and died in California.

FRANCIS, the oldest son, had ten children of whom two sons remained on the front road to carry on the Peck name — William Myron and Samuel Clifford. Will married Helen Drewery of Smithfield. She is a descendant of the family who once owned the haunted house which along with the mill was sold to Mirance Redner. They had three daughters, Olive, Mary, and Dorothy, all of whom are married and away from home.

CLIFFORD lives on lot eighty-six and the property for the red school house was taken from his farm. He married Greta Weese and their family consists of two boys, Beauford and Wayne. The former is on the farm with his father and married Ruth Williamson in 1939. They have several children now attending the Red school next door. These will be the sole remaining Pecks in the community in the coming generation. Wayne married Deanne Turkleboom in Belgium in 1946. They have one daughter.

WILLIAM, the third son of James Henry, built the brick house west of the church and had five daughters four of whom lived on the front road. Hattie, unmarried, occupies the homestead, Gertrude married Harry Anderson and had one daughter Mary who married Sherman Babbit. Blanche married Ernest Redner and had three sons, Carrol, Bernard and Keith; Florence married a Presbyterian minister, George Rowland and Grace married Earl Bonter and had four children, Eleanor who married Allan Weese, Harold, who married Evelyn Stephenson for his first wife and later Helen Miller. Evelyn married Howard Holmes and Joyce, unmarried, lives in Toronto.

JOHN GREER PECK married Nancy Jane Weese and had six children, the oldest being Samuel Pembroke, who along with brother Harry Woodruff cared for Albury cemetery for many years.

PEM. married Hessie Bryant and had a family of two daughters, Isobel who married Don Hatfield on Huff's Island and Dorothy who married John Albert Adams.

HARRY married Lena Sager in 1899 and their family also consisted of all girls — four in number. The oldest, Bernice married Lloyd Weese in 1920. She died in 1932. Lorna married Bill Bowerman in 1924, Myra married Robert Stephenson in 1932 and Marjorie is still at home.

Harry was born in February 1874. Like many of the older people of our time he could tell many interesting stories of the days before automobiles came into being and of the times the farmers did statute labour on the front road to keep it in repair.

* * *

Grandmother Peck, in the year of her death which took place in 1825, donated one acre of land for school and church purposes and to provide a burying ground for all protestant Christian denominations so long as they lived together in peace and harmony. Hitherto there had been no regular burying place in the district and in many cases the deceased had been laid to rest in a corner of some field usually on the back part of the farm where their rest should in no way be disturbed by passers-by other than those to whom their affections were held near and dear.

That lady must have been a shrewd business woman as she evidently left little to chance. After she had donated the ground for the church she meant that a church should be built, so she appointed the first seven trustees with the stipulation that none of them nor their descendants in office could be removed from a position as long as the dignity of the church was upheld.

The first church erected on the property was supervised by W. F. Weese who had also married a Weese as James Peck had married Elizabeth. This church was of stone construction and approximately only half the size of the present edifice and had a gallery in the north end or front which faced the road. Its seats were homemade by the men of those days with a tendency toward carpenter work and had two aisles in the centre and one on each side. Leo Fones played the organ for many years in the old church as well as several in the new and this transformation took place in 1898. By a strange coincidence Randal Weese's wife, Nancy Brickman, was the last funeral in the old church and Phoebe Weese, his mother, was the first one in the new one.

The school house stood a few feet to the west of the church on what ground is now part of the cemetery and was of frame construction but unfortunately was destroyed by fire some time in the sixties and was never rebuilt on that location due in all probability to the proximity of the burying ground. With the need for a new educational centre a great controversy arose between two factions of the section — those who lived on the hill and those who lived under the hill. The former demanded that the school be built on the top of the hill and the latter were equally strong in their demands that the school be built under the hill as any other location would be entirely unsuitable for the building. Finally a compromise was made and land was leased from W. T. Dempsey for a period of ninety-nine years and the school was built on its present location just under the hill. Miss Cork has taught the younger element at Albury for the past thirty years. W. T. Dempsey's wife was a Brickman — a sister of Alpheus of Centre.

As the property of the old school could not extend further to the west than the gift land provided for by grandmother Peck, the older people marvelled that the church, even though it may have been of stone construction, did not burn at the time of the destruction of the school. On frequent occasions extending to this day stones from the school foundation have been removed when graves were being dug where that building once stood.

The John G. Peck family

When the founders of the Peck settlement arrived in this country from the U.S.A. they were designated as Empire Loyalists and like so many of the others who retained their loyalty to the British crown had their property confiscated. The Pecks, like the Brickmans, always entertained the hope that at some future date their rights might be established to their heritage in New Jersey and on Manhattan Island and great care has been taken to preserve family records that might otherwise have been destroyed, but their hopes have been built on the sand and time and tide of the intervening years have eliminated any expectation of fortune that might have been entertained by any of the descendants of the original settlers.

Grandmother Peck proved her shrewdness in more ways than one because she outwitted the American authorities and brought most of her money with her. She knew that once she could get across the border with her American gold there would be no further worry about its ownership so she filled the bottom of a rather large tub with money and poured hot lard over it and this, to all intents and purposes was, at least as far as the immigration officials were concerned, food for her family. A marble slab designating her last resting place may still be seen in the cemetery — about fifty feet from the south end of the church, and I trust that this article will enlighten many of her descendants concerning her generosity and foresightedness and that all credit will be given to the one who made such provision for the future generations of her community.

There are few families today living within several miles of Albury Cemetery who cannot lay claim to having some of their loved ones lying beneath its sod.

The old church was torn down in the spring of 1898 and upon its demolition the construction of a new one was started immediately. When the roof of the old building was removed Will Peck, on a dare from some of the other men, walked up to the peak on one rafter and down the other side on another.

During the time taken for construction of the new church, services were held in Peck's hall, a building built by John Greer and located just west of Pem's house. Around this hall centred a great deal of the community life of the section and although the bottom part was used by the Pecks for a drive shed the upper storey was finished off with a hardwood floor and was used for parties and dances. Usually three or four dances were held there every winter and an orchestra from Belleville supplied the music. Its leader was an old German by the name of Chaulapke (spelling is not guaranteed on that name) who played the first violin while his daughter, Lulu played the piano. Bob Bland played cornet and Jack Weese, who sold monuments for years in the city played bass viol. James Gerow, father of Laurel (Ted) who was for years storekeeper in Rossmore, did the calling off and young people from all over the township came to the dances, usually in sleigh loads and tied their horses either in the Peck barn or in the church shed across the road.

The history of Albury and that of the Peck family have come hand in hand over the trail of the past century and a half. There must, however, be radical changes in the not too distant future when all the original holdings of the family and also the caretaking of the cemetery must pass into other hands.

Time continually creates changes on every hand but it cannot erase memories nor detract from a list of the many noble deeds of our forefathers on which must be given a place of high honour the names of James and Elizabeth Peck.

The Doxsee Family

I was sitting by the Doxsee kitchen table (somehow I always prefer a kitchen table) with a few books and papers before me looking into the family history of the settlers of that name and also of the community which derived its name from another family of United Empire Loyalists.

According to available records and I quote, "The original Archelaus Doxsee came from Long Island where his parents who were English had their home on the sound near Brooklyn. The English lived among the New Hollanders and intermarried with them so that both languages were in use and many members of the Doxsee family came to use Dutch as their language. The pioneer married Martha Rayser of Long Island and brought his family with him when he came to Canada in 1800. He journeyed north by way of the Mohawk valley and arrived at the St. Lawrence River a little above Clayton. He came up by way of Adolphustown but did not stop there, so crossed the bay and located at Green Point on the farm adjoining Cole's wharf. Green Point was settled earlier than the land that lay to the west toward Northport and among its earliest settlers were the Doxsee, Row, Shortt and Carman families.

SYLVANUS DOXSEE, son of the pioneer, married Elizabeth Shortt, daughter of Adam Shortt, a Prussian soldier whose original name was Adam Kurtz. They had nine children, the oldest of whom was named Adam Kurtz. An apprenticed weaver in his own country, disliking both his master and his trade he ran away to Hanover where he found agents recruiting soldiers to fight for King George III in his war with the American Colonies. He enlisted and so found his way to the western world. Peace having been declared he was given the option of returning to Europe or of taking up land in Canada. He chose the latter and located on the high shore where he acquired three hundred acres. With the very natural inclination to appear more British he had his name translated into Shortt.

The Doxsees are now numerous and have become prominent in many parts of the Bay of Quinte district, particularly in Hastings and Northumberland counties. John L., son of Adam K. and grandson of the original settler, was postmaster at Gilbert's Mills and served for years in Sophiasburgh council. He has been a member of the county council and reeve of the township. His father was born in 1811 and took up land in Sophiasburgh where the Doxsee farm is at present. Adam K. was twice married taking for his first wife Avon Parks and for his second Mary Dingman each of whom had a family of four children. John L. married Frances Tillotson of Mountain View. They had seven children — six girls and one boy. Frances married Arthur Tripp, Maude married Percy Oake, Pearl married Ernest Hubbs, Leah married Burton Pearsoll, Clema married Cecil Hayes and Blanche married Clark Sprung. Curtis was the only son, his name being the English version of the original Kurtz — this name along with that of Archelaus being carried down through the descendants of the original settler.

A prominent member of the family was Professor Egerton R. Doxsee, son of Rev. Archelaus and Alma VanDusen. He attended public and high schools of Port Hope and completed his education at Victoria University receiving the degrees of B.A. and B.D. and was for years professor of Classics at Albert College in Belleville.

The present owner of the Doxsee homestead married Bessie Mills who lived at West Lake — by the old wishing tree and she remembers many people stopping under the old landmark, many of whom were sweethearts who tarried long enough to make one wish which usually came true because they made it that way, but it was no novelty to her because nothing may be regarded as a novelty when it is situated almost on one's own door-step. Many had their pictures taken too in memory of a few thrilling moments spent under the spreading branches of the old tree and she remembered having hers taken just once — when she was in a group of children, part of whom stood on the rounds of a ladder and the larger boys sat on the lower limbs.

CURTIS DOXSEE and Bessie Mills have a family of three, the oldest being Leland who lives on a farm of his own a short distance from the homestead. He married Dorothy Huskisson and they have two daughters.

The Doxsee farm borders on and includes a section of what is known as the big swamp. The church and school house were not a part of the Doxsee property but were purchased from Peter Saunders and his wife Mary. The land was bought for the school in 1870 and fifty dollars was paid for approximately half an acre, the measurements of the deed being in chains. The present building is the third which has been used for educational purposes, the first being of log construction and set in the middle of what is now the swamp road. It was destroyed by fire and was replaced by a frame structure built on land rented for the purpose but purchased before the present school was built in 1873. S.S. No. 3 Sophiasburgh is situated on lot fifty-two in the second concession and the brick school was built by a man by the name of Lowder.

The church was built in 1871 and is the only one ever known as Doxsee's but there was another — a Presbyterian church on the first concession which was eventually closed and sold to W. R. Munroe and is at present in use as a drive shed on the Munroe farm. John L. Doxsee moved the building a mile to its present location with a steam engine. Doxsee's and Bethel churches were both built the same year and a double dedication service was held.

Curtis Doxsee has the distinction of being one of the land owners of Prince Edward County to hold a Crown deed to his farm which, of course, means that the family by that name started tilling the same soil back in the early part of the nineteenth century.

It has always been a credit to any lot of people when a church or school or hamlet has taken shape in those early years and been so called to perpetuate the name.

As the coming of David Demorest gave the world the name of Demorestville, so another family in the township of Sophiasburgh has made a worthwhile contribution to local history by the fact that their fellow citizens chose to do them honour through the establishment of a community carrying the name of Doxsee's.

The Sprague Family

The Spragues migrated from England early in the eighteenth century and settled on Long Island, New York, where three sons were born to the original settlers bearing that name. One came to Nova Scotia, another crossed into Rhode Island which was later governed by one of his descendants, and the third, Elijah remained on Long Island. He and his wife had three sons also, Samuel, Sylvanus and Elijah. The latter remained in the land of his birth but Samuel and Sylvanus were the pioneers of the family in Upper Canada.

SAMUEL settled on lot 28 on the first concession of Sophiasburgh not far from Northport. He was a shipbuilder by trade and had occupied a responsible position in the shipyards of Brooklyn before coming to Canada. He owned a schooner which had been leased to an unkown man without making proper inquiries concerning his integrity. The man engaged in contraband trade with the result that the ship was confiscated by the United States government. He had a schooner partly completed for himself at the time of his death.

Oak was plentiful on his farm and he frequently cut and squared timber which he rafted to Montreal and sold. He failed to return from one of these trips and was robbed of a thousand dollars which he had received for his timber. He is reported to have died of typhoid fever but it is not certain whether this was actually the case or whether he was murdered for his money.

SYLVANUS followed his brother to Canada, coming by way of Albany to Sackett's Harbour before crossing the river St. Lawrence. He and his family brought their possessions in a covered wagon which was so crowded that the women rode and the men walked — shooting what game they could along the way to supply their needs. He was greatly disappointed with the new country and when his teams had rested he made up his mind that he would return at once to his former home. He was a builder by trade and as some of his neighbours needed a skilled workman to assist with the erection of a house it was only natural that he rendered the necessary assistance. His success with that undertaking created such a demand for his services that before he realized it the season had advanced until it was too late to return before the cold weather set in. As a consequence he deferred his return to Long Island until the following autumn. When it was again time to make preparations for the journey he found that he had loaned a considerable amount of money that he had brought with him to several of his neighbours and could not get it back in time as their only security was wheat and it had to be threshed by treading it with horses, then taken to Kingston to be ground and finally shipped to Montreal to be sold as flour. Final payment to the grower was not made until the following May. As he could not afford to leave without the money, he took a homestead to work on shares from a settler by the name of Benjamin Smith.

Finally when events took the necessary turn and the opportunity arrived for him to put into effect his longing to return he decided that the ties in the new land were too strong to be severed. He remained in Sophiasburgh for twelve years and in 1832 he moved to Ameliasburgh.

SAMUEL SPRAGUE married Catharine Smith and they had eight children, Parmenus, Samuel, Daniel, Hallet, Smith, Hannah, Bishop and Reuben. Hallet married his brother Samuel's widow and they had six children, Parmenus, Louisa, Catharine, William H., John A. and George W. John A. married Ellen Badgley and settled on Big Island where one son, Grant was born. A daughter, Nellie, died at the age of eighteen. Grant married Maude Doney and they had four children, Mary Ellen, now Mrs. Howard Wallbridge, John Edward, Clarence and Jay.

JOHN A. always took a keen interest in public affairs and for fifteen years was a member of Sophiasburgh Township council, occupying not only that position, but deputy-reeve and reeve as well. He was elected to the Legislature as a Liberal in 1886 and was subsequently re-elected, serving in this capacity until 1894. While representing Prince Edward in the House he participated in the celebration of the centennial anniversary of the establishment of representative government in Upper Canada and received a medal with Lieutenant-Governor Simcoe's name on the one side while on the other was inscribed "Representative System Proclaimed, Kingston, July 16, 1792. First Parliament opened

Niagara Sept. 17, 1792. Centennial Celebration 1892." On the outer rim surrounding the above inscription was a further wording: "Upper Canada; since 1867 Ontario".

HALLET purchased lot No. 4 on Big Island and when legislation was enacted granting the powers of local government to municipalities he was elected a member of the first council of Sophiasburgh.

SYLVANUS and his wife had seven children: Lawrence, Elijah, Foster, George, Catharine, Sylvanus and Nostrand. The latter was only three years of age when his father migrated to Canada and he began his career as a clerk in Demorestville where he afterward operated a store of his own. Owing to ill health he turned to farming and specialized in growing hops to such an extent that he became known as the Hop King of Prince Edward. He also took an active interest in municipal affairs, being a member of the local council for seven years and reeve for six. He had the distinction of serving two terms as warden of the county.

AUSTIN SPRAGUE, second son of Lawrence, also served in the Sophiasburgh council from 1882 to 1886. He married Jane Mills and they had two children, Louise who married William Rightmyer, and Clayton who married Mabel Rightmyer.

GEORGE, the third son, married Jane Badgley and they had five children: Stanley, who remained on the homestead, Etta, Charles, James W. and Luella.

SYLVANUS JR. and his wife Eunice Huff, have also left many descendants in the district. John M. married Letty Giles and they had five children: Marcus, William G. (the doctor with the Hudson), Albro, Letty and Mary.

The second son, Elijah married Mary Williams and settled at Roblin's Mills. They had three boys: Douglas, Edward and Harry. Two daughters, Philana and Elizabeth were next in the family of Sylvanus Jr., while the third son, Lawrence S., married Jane Brickman and settled near Mountain View. Their children were Charles G., Lillian and Adelaide.

GEORGE married Adelaide Doolittle and also settled in Ameliasburgh. They had one daughter, Della, who married A. G. Roblin, the father of Ross and Rae who operate Roblin Dairy in Belleville.

Grant Sprague, founder of the Sprague Telephone Company, 1898

NOSTRAND had three children: Dr. James S., settled in Stirling; Albro was twice married, first to Harriet Baker and then to Nellie Beauchamp. A daughter, Minnie was born from the first marriage while Nostrand who has a summer home near the Carrying Place, was the only child from the second. The third child married Rev. R. Duke of the Bay of Quinte Methodist conference.

GRANT, the only son of John A., was a clever electrician and to him must go the credit of the founding of the Sprague Telephone Company in the upper part of the county.

The Sprague Telephone System

"Hello! Hello! I can't hear you. There are so many receivers down on this line that I can't hear a word. I do wish they would hang up."

Many of the subscribers on a party line have had exactly that experience at some time in their lives whether they be young or old. But the telephone, like the automobile, has become such a taken for granted commodity in this present age that few of us ever stop to give it a thought — except on very special occasions. In cases of emergency we rush for it, when we don't have it we feel that there is something amiss in our lives, when it doesn't work we curse it and in our weakest and wickedest moments we threaten to jerk it off the wall or tramp it into the floor if it happens to be a desk model but most of the time it is just our telephone to be used judiciously for business purposes and, I might go so far as to say, perhaps not quite so judiciously for pleasure. Too few of us, however realize the story behind the lines and the importance of those who work for the various companies to render John Public the service he needs and demands.

As soon as Grant Sprague had achieved a degree of young manhood he displayed his talents as an electrician and became interested in the telephone, eventually constructing a line from his home on Big Island to that of his uncle, James Longwell, some two miles distant. The first conversation was held on March 27, 1898. The two miles at that time was an almost incredible distance to talk because few of the residents of the countryside had ever seen a telephone and many visitors were admitted to witness its workings — some of whom had driven miles with old dobbin on the buggy or democrat.

Miss Lillian Sprague, who served over forty years in the capacity of secretary-treasurer of the company, recalled several amusing incidents of the early days. Many people conceived the idea that the strength of their voice alone could be responsible for its being able to carry such a long distance and the longer the distance the louder they shouted into the mouthpiece of that strange contraption hanging on the wall. She did not go far enough to mention the effect that it might have had on the ears of the switchboard operators, but that could be left to the imagination of the readers. The trials and tribulations of the first operators were many and varied. The story of one old lady, she laughingly told, when the mother of one of the line's first subscribers went to talk over the newly installed telephone. She was definitely in the near-sighted class and whenever she took down the receiver to answer, she would invariably call to some of the other members of the family to bring her her glasses so she could see who was on the other end of the line.

Switchboard operators in the Picton office, 1928

The present Sprague line is the third owned by the family, the first being developed from that first single line on Big Island which eventually became the People's Mutual System of Sophiasburgh. The care and upkeep of the line, however, became a case of that old adage "what is everybody's business is nobody's business", so after much difficulty had been experienced along this line, it was eventually absorbed into the Bell system. Then there was a second line in the township of Hillier operating mostly to the north and west of Wellington and with the central in Hillier village. That was in the time of the old horse and buggy days when quite too much time might elapse between a trouble call and a repair job. On this line the repair gang would leave home on Monday morning and often not return until Saturday afternoon. At its height of success the line boasted approximately one hundred subscribers. Mrs. Hardy kept central and one day a frantic call came to the Spragues for help. She had broken her receiver and could take no calls. Ordinary business did not worry her to such an extent but it was those emergency calls — a fire, accident, a sudden call for the doctor — would they please come and fix it as soon as possible ?

Today the efficiency of the service and maintenance are the highest on record. Rates have been advanced but costs have advanced accordingly and neither business nor farm can be looked upon as a successful institution today without a telephone. It has become part of our lives to such an extent that whatever may transpire in the future generation there can be no world without either a telephone or a yet unknown invention to create an improvement for individual communication.

In any event as the name of Alexander Graham Bell will be ever honored for his invention, so will the name of Grant Sprague be honored as the father of the independent systems in the north and western parts of Prince Edward County.

When the line was first started in Ameliasburgh the only previous telephone service was a few Bell phones spread over the entire area and most of these were owned by businessmen or occasionally a very prosperous farmer. Owen Roblin had one at Roblin's Mills and Stanley Potter had another at Mountain View where he ran the greenhouse and canning factory.

Grant bought the property in Mountain View where the exchange now is from Ed Hubbs who ran the store, but a short time after buying it from Byron Frederick. The latter drove one of old time peddling wagons around the countryside and accepted eggs as payment for groceries and dry goods. He bought the business from Wilfred Potter. Phoebe Thompson was the first storekeeper on the premises and a story is told concerning some of the neighbouring farmers who occasionally had a few boiled eggs left over from dinner and desired a change of diet for the evening meal. Accordingly the remnants of the boiled eggs were taken to the store and disposed of to Phoebe. The Spragues operated the store for a number of years but eventually discontinued it in favour of the telephone business and the canning factory.

The first secretary-treasurer of the telephone company was Grant's father, John A. Sprague, but after his death the position was taken over by Miss Lillian who still shoulders the responsibility of that office. Her father, Lawrence, was one of the original shareholders of the company but eventually sold his interest to Grant.

J. Sprague and his father, Grant Sprague

The first Sprague central was at their residence at Big Island, while the first switchboard in Ameliasburgh was at Ernest Redner's in Rednersville. Then it was moved to the home of Mack Lont in Centre neighbourhood where Mrs. B. L. Redner lives at present. It was then moved to Lawrence Sprague's where Annie Mae Salisbury and Myrtle Spencer were operators and after a short period was moved to its present location in 1913. The central call used to be three rings but this was afterward changed to one long. Then another important change was in the installation of the push-button which allowed only central rings to go to the switchboard and all others only on the line.

The greatest major expansion of the system took place in 1940 when the Mountain View airport was connected. It had its own local switchboard but all outside calls as well as long distance were taken care of by the Sprague central. All underground cables had to be laid in the port and this entailed months of labour.

Grant announced his resignation from active management in 1948 at a dinner dance at Tobe's County Gardens and invested the responsibility of the business upon the shoulders of his youngest son Jay. The feature of that dinner was a three-storey cake surmounted with a miniature telephone and appropriately decorated with the inscription in white icing, "1898-1948, 50th Anniversary, Sprague Telephone System".

Lighthouse on Main Duck Island in the late 1920's.

Main Duck Island Days of Rum Runners

There are two sets of islands which come under the Ducks classification in the eastern part of Lake Ontario. The Government of Canada owns False Ducks, three miles out from the southeastern extremity of Prince Edward County, while Main Ducks is nine miles further south and east and with a position of approximately forty-four degrees latitude is in close proximity to the International Boundary Line between Canada and the United States. The proximity has lent circumstances to stories of International intrigue over a period of time unequalled, perhaps, at any other point in the great dividing line between the two countries.

The tall tales of Main Ducks, however, recall a period much earlier than that of the rum runners of the late twenties.

In the early history of our young country a boat, conveying supplies and men, was purported to have started from Kingston for the relief of a garrison at York but ran into difficulties on its journey and was wrecked on the dangerous shoals of the south shore of the island either as a result of the lack of information concerning the navigation of those waters or a strong southeasterly wind. The ship carried not only a relieving garrison but also gold to pay the soldiers on their release from duty.

How many soldiers or sailors escaped that catastrophe is not known but it is known that many lost their lives. It is also known that a mass burial was conducted, the bodies being placed in a long trench such as one might expect after a bloody battle between two opposing armies. Human remains have been dug up periodically through the ensuing years, partly as a result of the still continuing search for the gold which tradition says is buried somewhere on the island and partly from the curiosity of mankind among whom, it could truthfully be said, was Wesley Thomas. The latter told an amusing story concerning an arrow he cut in a tree trunk one day while gathering some wood for use on cool nights in the kitchen stove. Two years later a visitor to Main Ducks came to the inevitable conclusion that the arrow pointed to the spot where the gold was buried so he came back in due time with a detector with which he covered the island but his search availed him only the bitter experience of failure in his attempt. On one occasion the keeper of the lighthouse uncovered the skeleton of what must have been a very large man because, he said, "His skull was large enough to fit right over my head".

The island itself remained under the jurisdiction of the Department of Indian Lands until July 14, 1905, when it was patented by the Crown and sold to Claude W. Cole for twelve hundred dollars. The Crown patent calls for seven hundred and forty acres but two of those were expropriated by the government in 1913 "for the erection of a lighthouse and a suitable dwelling for the keeper and his assistant". That dwelling was duly constructed and is today a double frame house with plenty of room for two families and enough land in the rear for a garden spot which has proven most useful, especially during that period since fishing around the island was largely discontinued after its purchase by John Foster Dulles in 1941 for a summer home. Mr. Dulles was Secretary of State in the Eisenhower administration, so had only a limited amount of time at his disposal and his visits to the island were somewhat irregular.

After the purchase of the island by Mr. Dulles it was declared an official port of entry — probably the least known and least used in the four thousand miles of border line between the two countries. Previously any American visitor either by plane or boat had been compelled to proceed to Kingston for a permit to enter the country to the north and then retrace the distance to the island with the return to the United States a duplication of that inconvenience.

The greater part of the activity of Main Ducks has been in the time of the Coles who purchased it mostly for fishing and farming but later it was also used as a convenience for rum runners carrying contraband liquor from the south shore of Prince Edward across the lake to an unknown destination.

The United States coast guard cutters were continually on the watch for these infringers of the law and not infrequently one was either caught or chased back across the International boundary which was and still is less than a mile south of the island. Liquor of every description was transported and on one particular occasion one of the larger boats limped into the harbour at Main Ducks with a cargo of beer which was carried in wooden boxes. These boxes in turn were placed in bran sacks — three in a sack as the boxes themselves would float, if the boats were cornered, sufficiently to make it advisable to jettison their cargo. With the sacks, however one might still escape the clutches of the law because once overboard they would take in sufficient water to ensure the fact that they would no longer be floating on the top of the water. Just how much liquor lies on the bottom of Lake Ontario no one will ever know but it must be a sizeable amount. Mr. X, owner of the boat in question, had a thousand sacks in the hold of his craft but he was not to be daunted by a crippled ship. He owned two boats — one much smaller — so, as a natural conclusion, the thought immediately occurred to him that the other one, though much smaller, was much speedier and, while it would be necessary for him to risk the vigilance of the coast guard not once but ten times, he would take the chance.

Unfortunately for him his initial effort ended in utter disaster. The vigilant boats of the coast guard pounced on him on his very first trip across and he was taken to the mainland where, according to the usual procedure, his boat and cargo were confiscated and for his part in defiance of the laws of the country he was sentenced to five years of penal servitude. So nine hundred sacks of Canadian beer lay in the hold of the ship during the winter months unclaimed and as Mr. Wesley Thomas, lighthouse keeper on Main Duck Island for thirty-three seasons, expressed it "There were five of us on the island for at least part of that time and not one of us drank". The next spring, however, the beer as well as the ship disappeared.

An old saying gives the information that there is a certain amount of honour even among thieves. If that might have been the case in the rum running business the owner may have been recompensed to some degree for his loss. If, on the other hand, the opposite be true then there was one cargo of beer to which the owner could make no legitimate claim but resulted in a profit to a fellow rum runner which might run close to an amount necessitating four figures. That is, of course, if he had the good fortune to elude the law or if he had not previously paid too high a price for protection so that he might be free to dock his cargo of fish or some other commodity which must be regarded as legitimate and not interferred with in any way by enforcement officers of the United States Government.

"King" Cole Rules His Island Kingdom

Claude Cole was born and brought up at Milford in the lower part of the county and the possibility of success in cattle raising and fishing first led him to Main Duck. Mrs. Cole moved to the island to join her husband when their oldest son, Cecil was six months of age and she remained there for eleven years. Cecil died soon after he left Main Duck in 1921 and his younger brother, Wilmot died two years later while working on a government project in Deseronto.

Their father was nicknamed "King Cole" for his several successful enterprises which included the sale of timber from the island, cattle raising, horse racing, fishing and lastly but not least rum running. It was reported that at the height of his career he had amassed a fortune of well to a quarter of a million dollars. Though his interests were divided among these ventures the least profitable, to all appearances, was that of farming. He owned a string of race horses with which he amassed a sizeable amount on the tracks in the United States but was eventually suspended by the racing commission of the State of New York for running a horse under an assumed name. He appealed the case and after lengthy litigation finally lost. Several other cases of a various nature cut largely into personal income and this coupled with the family's station of living reduced their fortune still further.

During his period of prosperity he purchased a farm at Cape Vincent in New York State and spent the winters there rather than on Main Duck or back home in Milford.

The original residence built by the Coles burned to the ground in the spring of 1922 and was the only fire ever recorded on the island. They immediately replaced the house which was of frame construction. The new house was not built on the old foundation but the latter was reinforced by an eighteen-inch solid wall which, with the addition of a good roof, could be used for storage of milk and butter. In later years it was used for an ice house.

Three barns used to house the cattle had not been in a first class state of repair for many years and after the exit of the Coles from the island they gradually settled to the point of falling down and the lumber was burned as it was considered unfit for further use. Their cattle, once the mainstay of their sustenance on Main Duck, were disposed of and taken to the mainland ten at a time in their fishing tug and by the time the island had changed hands the horse population had been reduced from a dozen head including race horses to two which were used by the new owner to draw up a small amount of wood, fill the ice house or for any bit of work out of the range of human effort.

If the Coles accumulated a fortune on Main Duck it was dissipated quite as quickly as it was gained. C. W. Cole and his two sons passed on within a few years of each other and occupy a last resting place in Glenwood Cemetery. In the final analysis the farm at Cape Vincent was disposed of; the fish tug was no longer seaworthy and their island stronghold was sold to Mr. Dulles so all that is left to the memory of the Cole family in the neighbourhood of their activities is the house on Main Duck containing a small bit of furniture and a piano.

On one occasion the senior Cole was spending a night in Trenton. His tug was in the harbour and the next morning before he loosed his moorings two drays of furniture arrived at the dock and the drivers began to transfer their loads to the ship owned by Mr. Cole. "What's the idea?" asked the owner of the tug.

"It was brought here on your orders sir", came the answer.

"Never even heard tell of it", replied Mr. Cole. "There must be a bad mistake somewhere. I may have celebrated a little last night but I did not go in the furniture business."

"You bought the works from the bar in the hotel", the drayman told him "and you not only bought it you paid cash for it and ordered delivery to be made to the tug."

So the furniture, including a piano, was loaded on board ship and transported to Main Ducks. There is neither legend, or hearsay concerning that story because Wesley Thomas helped move the load from the tug to the house. The bar, which was about ten feet wide was thrown out and burned but the piano is still in the house and in very good state of repair.

And what of Main Duck before the regime of the Coles? Since I first became interested in the island's history that question has been in the back of my mind and the answer came at a most unexpected time and from a most undeniable source. One day while conversing with Jim Hepburn mention was made of the Coles and their island kingdom.

"The governor", [his father] said Mr. Hepburn, "rented that island from the government for many years for the very nominal sum of sixteen dollars a year. I have often wondered since why he did not buy it. He used to pasture some cattle and a few sheep out there but kept mostly hogs. He never fed them anything and they would grow up during the season eating grass, the entrails of the fish which the fishermen would cast away, and blacksnakes. Somehow no one has ever been able to explain it, a snake has a fascination for a hog and the hogs would go down to the water's edge and eat them as fast as they would appear."

I inquired how the pork might taste on such a diet and as all this happened over half a century ago we are quite free to express an opinion that it might have been a bit fishy.

The old road past Eatonville

Eatonville

First of all I shall have to turn back the years and invite you to come with me on an imaginary trip to sometime early in the last century when a man by the name of Norris Bristol erected a building on lot seventy-six, Township of Ameliasburgh in the edge of what is most commonly known to all of us as "the marsh". It was probably located partially on or almost on land where the road now is.

The Bristols were of U. E. L. descent. John, the progenitor of the Bristol family of Prince Edward County was born in Albany, New York, where he married Alice Aylesworth. Soon after the revolutionary war he moved to Ernesttown in Lennox County where he and his wife raised a family of five sons — John, Coleman, Benjamin, Norris and Joel. Somewhere about 1819 Benjamin established a tannery about a mile east of Picton where he resided and which was the first or one of the first to be established in Prince Edward County. Benjamin's oldest son started a clothing store in Picton which, in later years became one of the leaders of its kind in the district — A. Bristol & Son — while Norris moved to Ameliasburgh and started a tannery on the borders of a marsh flowing through that township. Somewhere around the year of 1845 he disposed of the business to William G. Stafford who already had become established in farming within sight of the business.

The Staffords came to Canada from Ireland — from the County of Tyrone in the northern part of the country and the original settler was a weaver by trade, having been a foreman in an establishment of that nature in his native land. John Stafford came to Canada as a young man and first settled in Picton where he was employed as a clerk in one of the town's leading dry goods stores at the time. During the period of his employment with McAllister and Ballard, sometime around 1826 he married the only daughter of Richard and Mrs. Gardner. Richard Gardner was the owner of a brewery in the county which carried the family name. Shortly after his marriage he purchased a farm on the second concession of Spohiasburgh near where the church now is at Mount Pleasant. He died in 1837, the year of the William Lyon Mackenzie rebellion but had been previously commissioned by the governor, Sir Francis Bond Head, to transport men to Toronto who had been drafted to serve in helping quell the rebellion. He assisted in the building of the old Conger Chapel, a short distance from Picton on the Demorestville Road and his remains rest peacefully in the cemetery there to this day.

First of the John Eatons, I am told, came originally from near Dover in Kent County, England and settled in New England before coming to Canada. John Sr. and his wife were of United Empire Loyalist stock and had thirteen children among whom were John Jr., Jacob and Isaac. Another brother of John Sr. emigrated from Ireland and his son, Timothy, became the founder of that mighty merchandising empire which reaches completely across this great country today and carries the name of The T. Eaton Co., Ltd.

Isaac, John and Jacob were United Empire Loyalists and the latter was given a grant of a hundred acres of land in Tyendinaga Township near Melrose in Hastings County. Though he had three wives there were never any children and, on his demise, John took over the farm. He was credited with an inventive mind and had several inventions to his credit but he passed on without heirs so, as a result, the surviving brother was left in possession of the farm. Isaac's full name was Isaac Robinson Eaton but he always went by his initials rather than by name so when anyone spoke of I. R. little explanation was necessary. He was gifted with considerable musical talent and frequently fulfilled the position of lay preacher which he could always be depended on to do in case of emergency.

However he was not a farmer at heart and started a boot and shoe business in Stirling which he operated for several years. During many of those days money was very scarce and, according to his accounts, a considerable amount of his business was transacted by the barter system as he would accept produce from the farm at any time in exchange for any of his goods in the store. He married Abigal Way, whose people were also of U. E. L. descent and the Ways in the lower part of the county today are direct descendants of her family. They had eight children, four of whom never attained maturity, while the other four were Blanche, the eldest who married Will Rayfield, Ethel who married Wilbert Osborne, James — better known as Jim — who married Hannah DeLong while she worked as a domestic in the Stafford family when the Eatons took over the tannery while Frank, the youngest, went to New Jersey and married May Westerfield who was organist in the church in Morristown where he sang in the choir. He eventually made music his career and became widely known for his ability as a soloist. His wife was a very prim person while their only daughter was quite the opposite and never, or so it seemed, lost an opportunity to cause a bit of embarassment to her mother. During my early years as a very amateur photographer I remember taking her picture holding a little squealing pig and having a fine lark much to the consternation of her mother.

Will Rayfield was chef at the Hotel Quinte in Belleville for a number of years while Wilbert Osborne operated the farm in Massassaga where George Flower lives now. Jim was engaged in the garage business on the market square in Belleville for some time in partnership with his brother-in-law Milton DeLong.

After having spent some years in the business in Stirling, I. R. Eaton conceived the idea of going into the manufacturing business so he purchased the tannery from the Staffords and one winter's day he set out with his family and by means of horses and sleighs came south across the ice of the Bay of Quinte with all his worldly possessions and not only fulfilled his original dream but started a village as well as a tannery business and that place became known as Eatonville which, although a ghost village today, perpetuated the name in this district and even today we occasionally hear its location spoken of as Eatonville.

During the meantime William G. Stafford, the eldest of the family, moved to Ameliasburgh in 1845 when he purchased the tannery from Norris Bristol and operated a profitable business for some years. That, of course, was previous to the time when Eatonville received its name as that was not to take place until his years of ownership had come to an end and the property sold to the Eaton family. The Staffords then branched out in another industry on lot seventy-eight which had previously been purchased from Alpheus Brickman and started growing and drying hops for the brewing trade. As the scene of its activities was less than a quarter of a mile away we will talk more about it a little later — that is after we have paid a visit to the tannery and the old blacksmith shop across the road.

During the era of the tannery the hides were purchased mostly in Prince Edward County but if supplies became short further purchasing might be done beyond its borders. They were scraped and placed in vats of which there were four large ones and it was endeavoured to keep these full at all times to ensure a constant supply of leather for the tannery.

The original method of making liquor for the tanning process was to gather hemlock bark and grind it with a machine run by horsepower where the horse kept going round and round until the days work was finished and the next day the same thing all over again — a bit of a monotonous job even for a horse. By the original method it took nearly a year to complete the cycle of tanning — that is from the time the bark was gathered until the finished product was taken from the vats. Eventually, however, the Eatons turned to a different process when they used liquor made from wheat which cut the time of processing to an average time of a month. The leather from the local tannery was used for making harness for the horses as well as boots and shoes — mostly boots in those days when long legged leather boots were quite fashionable — for men. If one wanted a robe made or a deer hide tanned it had to be taken to another tannery as the Eatons did not have the facilities to handle this kind of business.

When the hide was eventually done it would be split into two or three layers according to its ultimate use as the hides were much too thick for ordinary boots. One of the specialties of that time — and fashions changed in those days as they do today — was copper-toed boots for children. That is they would use a regular copper toe cap in their making. When Ralph Stafford told me of that style I misunderstood him to a certain extent and suggested that the kids would have to see to it that they behaved in a much better manner than those of today or the copper-toed boot might be brought into play on certain occasions of bad behaviour, but he assured me that they were built only for children. All the boots were custom made and one day a chap came in to order a pair and the measurements were taken but after the boots were received he came back and assured Mr. Eaton that they did not fit. Whereupon that gentleman in a single glance saw the difficulty, so he said to the dissatisfied customer that he had them on the wrong feet. The latter might not have been the most intelligent person in the world but he scored a point when he replied to Mr. Eaton, "Well these are the only two feet that I got."

I spent part of an afternoon with Mrs. William Ormond who was a granddaughter of the Eatons and who was able among other things to tell me the following story: She had forgotten his name but for convenience sake we will call him Charlie. Now Charlie loved to hunt above almost anything but usually he wasn't satisfied to use proper discretion on what he shot but if a bird of any description came in his way that bird was just about as good as a dead duck as he was a crack shot. One day I. R.'s son Jim, who was a bit of a prankster, said to Charlie that there was a big crane out in the marsh and if he had his gun handy he might get it. So he rushed in and got his gun and knocked over the bird with the very first shot. But the game was too far out in the marsh to wade to so Charlie excitedly hurried to the neighbours and borrowed a boat to retrieve his prize. One can quite imagine his chagrin when he discovered that he had been tricked. That bird was the one that I. R. Eaton had had stuffed and it had been in the front room as a decoration for so many years that it had become moth-eaten.

The liquor in the vats had to be stirred by hand and the one who had the job also had to be on guard as one day some of the boys took one of the planks that he had to walk over, sawed the bottom nearly in two and as a result down went a man into the tanning tank. Yes there were several methods of tanning hides in those days. I used to get mine tanned on the odd occasion but that was years later and was accomplished by an altogether different process.

Ralph Stafford told me that, as a young man, he used to have "quite an eye" for Blanche Eaton and on more occasions than one took her down to visit her uncle and aunt in Melrose. On one of his projected trips he tied his horse to the hitching post, which was the common thing to do in those days and when he went to untie it the pesky thing pulled back, got loose and ran away. So that trip had to be cancelled but on most other occasions he had better luck. On one of the weekends the two young people picked up a friend of the young lady in question and the three of them attended the Catholic church service in Read. That was the first of its kind he had ever attended.

One of the children of the family of I. R. Eaton and his wife died while they still resided in Eatonville and William Stafford hitched the team of horses on the hop wagon and took all the kids in the neighbourhood to the funeral.

Then there was the village itself. How things have changed since that time when there were no automobiles, there were no paved roads and the lady of the house did her washing over the board and tub or had a washing machine that she had to run by hand if she were lucky enough to own one at all, and did the entire amount of cooking for the whole family on the old wood stove and, for the most part, baked her own bread as well. That was the lot of Abigal Eaton who, not only did all this for her husband and four children but boarded most of the tannery help as well. They lived in a house directly across the road from our own and at about the time the tannery was closed, two families made it their dwelling — the Eatons and Jay Zufelt and his wife. It was not due to the fact that a market was lacking for the sale of boots and harness that was the deciding factor in the Eatons finding dificulties in continuing the business but modern methods of manufacture were beginning to make very large inroads in the business and price-wise they found they could not compete so, on his brother's death in Melrose, the Eaton family moved down there and for a number of years operated the farm that had been left to them as a legacy. I. R. operated the farm until he passed on and, as a posthumous tribute to him from the people of Rednersville, they asked that his funeral service be conducted from the local church there. This was granted and the edifice was filled to capacity for the service. If one cares to take the time to browse through the cemetery at Albury there is one tombstone which could scarcely escape attention entering the gate — one prominently bearing the name of Isaac Robinson Eaton.

The Redner house on the old Eatonville Road (now Highway 23)

His son, Jim took over the farm after his father's death but eventually sold it and went into the garage business in Belleville with his brother-in-law, Milton DeLong. Jim and Hannah Eaton had two children — Percy, who died from tuberculosis while still a young man — a disease he contracted while working in the mines of northern Ontario. A daughter, Lulu married Claude Wallace who was engaged for many years in the taxi business in Trenton and it is through her memory coupled with some research that I have the pleasure of presenting to you much of the information concerning Eatonville.

After the demise of the tannery business the building was used for a time as a blacksmith shop by Jay Zufelt but in later years stored only a few of the lesser used farm implements belonging to B. L. Redner who owned the place until he came to an unfortunate end by being choked to death when his dog inside the cab of his truck disengaged the lever holding up the dump while he was doing some greasing on the driveshaft. But, as time passed, the roof began to leak and then sag in the middle so the building fell into disuse and it deteriorated until only a part of its four walls remained intact. These were bulldozed down to make way for a new road during the summer of 1968 and some of the workmen told of seeing bits of leather from the years gone by but, unfortunately, we were in Europe that summer and missed the whole procedure. It was indeed unfortunate that we could not have shared in the discovery.

Before Jay Zufelt opened the blacksmith shop, however, there stood another just to the south of where our house now stands — as a matter of fact when digging in the flower garden there I have often dug up bolts or pieces of iron which could, if they were able to convey the message, relate many of those experiences of the blacksmith shop on the corner.

The proprietor of this shop was Levi Peters whose wife's name was Lucretia. She was apparently a bit difficult to get on with so the boys nicknamed her "electricity". The shop was set up on stilts or piles about two feet high as the water often overflowed the road at this point and the whole place accordingly would be flooded. A ramp was constructed to take the horses up to the level of the floor which was covered with hardwood plank. All the farmers did their work with horses at that time, their shoes being made at the shop and it cost a dollar to get a horse fitted out with a whole new set. The coming of more modern methods once again made this way of doing unprofitable so shoes were eventually all purchased and, inevitably the price of shoeing advanced accordingly. Peters also had a small barn down the side road leading to the Spencer farms with a windmill on the top where he ground grain for a limited number of farmers in the vicinity.

There was also a house further down the road where a family by the name of Fournyea lived and their children went to school at Centre. They were of French descent.

As for our own house — the only surviving memory of Eatonville — one finds it necessary to look back many years in a changing world to the time when Henry P. Redner received ownership of the property largely through a promise made by his father, Peter Redner who had bought a tract of ninety-three acres from his brother Henry Jr. who was listed in the deed as a tavern keeper in Rednersville. The latter was the son of the original Henry who first settled the north shore of Ameliasburgh township and perpetuated his name when the village received the name by which it is now known.

What might be described as a sale in trust was dated October 27, 1846 which conveyed the "lands and premises" to Lewis Redner and by a subsequent deed under date of November 26, 1869 Henry P. Redner received full ownership of the property for the nominal fee of one dollar. To achieve this all the members of the family had to "sign off" on a deed which was drawn up in 1872 and which contained the names of William Redner, Lewis Redner, Rinerd Redner, the latter being the grandfather of the writer, Mary (Aunt Polly) Ainsworth, Sophia Burr, mother of Dr. W. K. Burr, Naomi Way who was a widow, and Sarah Jane Stafford whose husband William owned and operated the tannery prior to the coming of the Eatons. The document was witnessed by Benjamin Brickman and Owen Roblin, both pioneers of their line, as being justices of the peace.

Henry P. kept the property but a short time and sold it later to Levi Peters, the blacksmith. It changed hands several times within the next thirty years as the latter sold it to a Mrs. Crouter and took a mortgage for three hundred dollars for two years with interest at ten percent. That was the entire purchase price but it seems that she could not make her payments and Peters repossessed the property and again sold it in 1890 to William Wright who kept the bees. He in turn sold it to George and Emma Redner but after a short duration of possession it was again sold to William Lont who held it for four years when it was purchased by my father, David Redner, in 1901 for four hundred dollars. For several years his sister, Adelaide who had never married, made it her home and then after her passing it was used as a house for the hired man of the farm until it became occupied by its present owners. During that time many changes have taken place, even the road that carries the traffic past our door which has been moved a hundred feet to the west, paved and is now known as County Road No. 23.

It probably takes in land where once stood a large house and which housed the Bristols and in later years it was divided to accommodate two families, one being James Eaton, son of Isaac and the other occupied by Jay Zufelt who ran a blacksmith shop for a time after the closing of the tannery.

One of my articles published in the *Picton Gazette* was entitled "The Farm Just up the Road" which at the time was occupied by Jim and Winifred Stavely and which was the old home of the Staffords after they left the tannery in the hands of the Eatons. It was here that they added to an already established industry in the county — hop growing. At that time the largest growers in the county were Cooper and MacDonald of Hallowell Township who also acted as buyers or agents of buyers in larger cities and bought the entire crop not only from the Staffords but also John Howell and his brother, Jim who lived next to the mountain on the lower second concession of Ameliasburgh. The hops when sufficiently dried, were put in bales of two hundred pounds and were shipped to Montreal either for use there or for reshipment to the United States for the brewing of beer.

The Staffords started out with a field of ten acres. The plants were obtained from suckers cut from the root of the parent plant so, once the industry was started it was not by any means difficult to obtain new shoots as each spring all the suckers had to be cut out whether they were used for new plantations or destroyed, for a single plant was left to produce the crop. My only recollection of the hop business is a pile of disused poles standing on end in the corner of a field once used for the purpose of growing the crop. Wellington Howell of the Howell plantation told me that once in a very heavy windstorm they lost a thousand poles in just over an hour, as these were all cedar, it meant a great loss and all had to be replaced before the plant could attain its growth. After each plant was set a hole was made beside it by using a spade and then a sharpened pole was jabbed into the ground and as soon as growth started the vine was tied to the pole which it entwined during the season's growth. After this operation was completed, usually as soon as danger of frost was over, a very rapid growth ensued and a second tie was made when the plant had attained a growth of four or five feet. This was repeated twice before the end of the season, the final tie being completed by horseback. The Howells had a horse that became so proficient in his line of duty that he stopped at every plant without even a word of instruction from his owner.

The time of harvest, as is usual with all farm produce, was the busy time of the year. This period usually lasted from two to three weeks. William Long collected the women — as many as fifty on good harvest days — with the team and wagon and did so for the duration of the harvest. The method of this gathering differed widely from any ordinary product as the plant was cut off approximately a foot above the ground, the pole pulled out and carried to the end of the field where one could see a row of boxes and the women busily picking the product from the plant. Each box had four sections and each section held about seven bushels. A fair day's work for a picker would be one box for which she would receive thirty-five cents. Seventy cents was the top wages paid. A good crop produced six to seven hundred pounds per acre and, at the peak of the prices dried hops sold at a dollar a pound. The average over a period of years was fifty cents and when the price eventually fell to forty the business was no longer considered profitable and, as a result was discontinued.

When the boxes were filled in the field they were emptied into large burlap sacks and taken to the drying room to be placed over heat the following night. This part of the business was never trusted to outsiders but was looked after invariably by the owners themselves because there was no market for hops once they had been scorched. The Staffords did their drying on the second floor of a building built for the dual purpose of drying hops and housing their buggies and machinery, the former occupying possibly the larger part of the upstairs while considerably less space was used on the ground floor for here was mainly the source of their heat which was generated by a huge box stove. This was eventually sold to heat Holloway United Church (then Methodist) in Belleville and was eventually sold from there and brought back to warm the young hopefuls of Centre School.

The heating floor was covered with a very heavy type of lath with spacings left for the warm air to infiltrate and this, in turn, was covered with either the heavy burlap sacks or a type of very fine wire mesh to prevent the hops from sifting through. Sulphur was used as a bleeching agent to prevent the finished product becoming discoloured during the process of drying and the hops had to be turned every hour until they would be reduced to the moisture required for shipment. The stalks and leaves were piled in a convenient spot in the corner of the field where they might be burned when they became sufficiently dry. A forkful of stable manure was placed over each root partly as a protection against the elements through the winter and also for the purpose of fertilizing the plant for the coming season.

The shipments of both barley and hops, which commodities had moved in large quantities from our county, began to dwindle at about the same time and the price declined for both, forcing the growers to turn to other crops for a source of income and today the growing of hops is a forgotten industry and the commodity of barley is grown only for the purpose of feed for the livestock.

Time may have erased the fact that either could be looked upon as a profitable enterprise, the tempo of life may have completely changed from those horse and buggy days but one characteristic still remains to the fore in the thoughts of mankind — the idea of exploring the unknown. Eve sought to take advantage of such a situation when she partook of the forbidden fruit in the garden of Eden. As I sat in the Staveley kitchen going over some points of my article the young son arrived home from school with a very perplexed look on his face and sought the answers to his questions which went something like this:

"Mother, how old will I be in the year 2000?"

"Let me see," was the answer — "you are nine now; that would make you fifty-seven."

"How old will Lloyd be?" (Lloyd was his chum at school.)

"He is six months older than you are. He will be fifty-seven for part of the year and fifty-eight for the rest".

"How old will you be mother?"

"Oh," she answered with an unmistakable twinkle in her eye, "I will still be twenty-five".

"What will the world be like then?"

"That's a real toughie, son. You've got me stopped there. I'm afraid I haven't got an answer for that one".

The old tannery at Eatonville

The Conger Family

DAVID CONGER was born at Piscataqua, N.J., in 1791. He was a brass founder and a silversmith by trade and after the close of the Revolutionary War he settled on a small farm in Ulster County, New York State.

Loyalty to the Crown rendered his position unpleasant after the establishment of the new republic and in 1786 he came to Hallowell and purchased a lot with a mill site two miles east of Picton. The next year he returned for his wife and family and brought with him irons and castings for a saw mill which he had in operation before the close of 1787. His next enterprise was to build a grist mill as the pioneers, up to that time, had to take their corn either to Kingston or Napanee to have it ground. Many were the dangers as they either went by canoe, drove across the treacherous ice in the winter or even carried the sacks on their backs when they were unable to avail themselves of any other method.

The strong religious tendencies of David Conger led him always to keep in mind the interests of his church. He was a strong adherent of Methodism and one of his gifts to that body was a site on his lot for a church which in later years became known as the Conger Chapel. It was erected in 1809 and is now the oldest Methodist church in continuous use in what was then Upper Canada. There is an older one at Hay Bay but this building has had other uses than that of a church.

When David Conger came over with his family, his ninth child, Stephen, then a lad of fourteen helped to drive the cattle and it is said that he spent nearly a month on the road coming north. Stephen grew into a man of importance in the land of his new home. At the early age of thirty he was appointed Justice of the Peace and was one of the first magistrates of Prince Edward County. Among the duties of a magistrate in those days was that of legalizing marriages. Although many ministers were licensed to publish the banns of the contracting couples they were not legally qualified to unite them in marriage. Those couples, accordingly, would have to appear before the Justice of the Peace who would perform the marriage ceremony. Stephen Conger solemnized seventy-six marriages between 1803 and 1823. The brown envelope handed me by Ed. Brawley contained these records intact in Stephen Conger's own handwriting.

He was not only regarded as a man of high moral standing in his community but he was endowed with a strong intellectuality. He was invariably offered a seat on the bench when the circuit judges held assize. It was the custom of that body to invite one or two well qualified men of the district to confer with them respecting local customs, boundaries, disputes, waterways, etc.

He also took a keen interest in electricity when that science was still unkown to the settlers and his wife went so far as to make the statement that he must be out of his mind to waste time on such a trivial matter.

No records are available to tell just how he met his wife but a story is told that his proposal was made to Mary Bates by sending a note all the way from Picton to Cobourg by a special messenger on horseback. That he received a favourable answer was proven by the fact that his wife, Mary Bates, bore him eight children, seven of whom attained maturity.

The old pioneer, David Conger, left many descendants in the Prince Edward district but the name of Conger, like so many more of the old pioneer names, is rapidly becoming only history. The only living residents carrying the family name living in the district today are Stephen B. and his sister Alice who at present reside on North Bowery Street in Picton.

The name of Stephen has been a favourite in the Conger families, for not a generation has passed without adding one more member of the descendant families by that name.

NANCY LANGHORN the eldest daughter and first child of the magistrate and his wife, married John P. Roblin. Mrs. W. H. R. Allison is a direct descendant.

DAVID STODDARD, grandfather of Stephen B. and Alice, married Elizabeth Benson. He took up two hundred acres of land near Owen Sound for each of his sons — Stephen B., Nelson Bates, Roger David, William Manley and James A., but none of the second generation remained there and the property all passed into other hands. Stephen B. married Eliza Bolton and this couple were the parents of the present residents of the town.

ROGER B., second son of the magistrate, became a member of Parliament for the county but owing to laxity in the operation of his personal business did not attain the financial success of his brother David Stoddard. He married Hannah Bryant of Ameliasburgh.

RACHEL married Anthony Herrington and lived in Ameliasburgh. Their grandson was W. S. Herrington, K.C., of Napanee who was extremely well known throughout the whole Bay of Quinte district. To add a personal note Walt. Herrington got his early education at our local seat of learning, S.S. No. 7, Ameliasburgh and sat in the seat with my father when he started school.

HULDAH S. married Owen Roblin. The latter figured very prominently in articles a couple of years back on Roblin's Mills as he was the industrial magnate of the village at that time.

ELIZA B. married Rev. Daniel McMullen whose sons were at one time owners of the Prince Edward Railway.

MARY G. married Peter Brickman and also settled in Ameliasburgh. A third son, Stephen died at an early age.

DAVID S., a brother of Stephen the magistrate, married Julia Owens and settled in Hallowell. They had eight children one of whom, John O., was the father of John W. who at one time was associated with the *Picton Gazette.* The ownership of the land where the golf club now is, still rested with the Conger estate when purchased by the club. Another grandson of David S., E. Marshall Conger, was also associated with the *Gazette.* Wilson S., son of Peter D. and grandson of the pioneer David, settled in Peterborough and was elected to parliament on several occasions for the county and eventually became its sheriff.

In addition to Stephen B., son of David Stoddard, there was Nelson Bates who married Melissa Cronk. He died while on the property near Picton and his widow moved to Toronto. Roger David married Adeline Brickman and all his three children have also crossed the Great Divide. One daughter, Bessie, married Geo. A. Kingston, a Toronto lawyer. James A. married Elizabeth Dempsey of Albury. He lived in Belleville for a time but afterward moved to Ottawa. Karl B., the youngest of his family, is the only surviving son. William Manley married his sister-in-law, the widow of Stephen B. after the latter's death. One daughter, Hester, married David Bryant.

WILLIAM MANLEY, who married Stephen's widow, conducted a nursery business for years on the property next to the site of the chapel. He learned the business in Syracuse and raised apple and fruit trees as well as grapes and many other lines of nursery stock. He, like many of the modern firms, had agents on the road selling his stock. The boys had all left home before their stepfather died suddenly of a heart attack in 1909 and his sudden passing left Alice and her mother in possession of a business which they were unable to continue so it was sold and the house on Bowery Street was purchased.

Conger Chapel, built in 1809

The Conger Chapel

It was an extremely cold day when I paid my first visit to the old church on the corner where the road leaves the high shore and starts westward to Demorestville. I did wonder what might have been in the back of the minds of some passers-by who saw a stranger on his knees in front of the various tombstones writing on a pad of very white paper. Those old tombstones might have held my interest still further on a day that was more conducive to my efforts but I did remain long enough to make the necessary notes and realize that this was truly the last resting place of many members of the Conger family.

DAVID CONGER, who is buried directly behind the Chapel, departed this life on January 9, 1816, at the age of fifty-five years while his wife, Juliana, attained the ripe old age of eighty-seven.

STEPHEN, the magistrate, did not live long to enjoy the fruits of his labours for he passed on on the 27th of April, 1827, at the early age of 54. On his tombstone is the following inscription:

A tender husband's eyes fast closed in death;
A loving father has resigned his breath.
My children mourn and with me fell the stroke
For cruel death has our connection broke.

Although the resting places of these people occupy the ground directly behind the Chapel, many other descendants are also buried in the yard at the rear of the church. Rachel, wife of Anthony Herrington, died when she was nineteen years and six months old. Other names in the cemetery include Arthur Youmans, Jacob Merrell, Abraham and Sarah Peterson whose deaths are recorded on the same day, October 12th, 1860, Jacob Benson, John Carley and Richard Gardiner. More recent stones carry the names of Cole, Coolidge, Gerow, Carr, Wood, Rickman, VanHorn, Kent, Jinks and Morden. This list is by no means a complete one.

The outside of the Chapel is in a wonderful state of preservation and gives one the impression of a much more modern structure. With its carefully tended yard and general exterior appearance it is difficult indeed to realize that this was one of Upper Canada's pioneer places of worship.

The deed for the Chapel property which is framed and hung on its wall reads in part—

> Stephen Conger of the Township of Hallowell in the County of Prince Edward in the Midland District and Province of Upper Canada
>
> and
>
> Stephen Conger, Helebrand Valleau, Henry Johnson, Abraham Van Blaricom, James Dougall, Jacob German, Jacob Benson, James Wilson and Casparus Vandusen.
>
> Beginning at the north-east angle of a post planted at the intersection of the Highways in front and that which cometh from the second concession Carrying Place . . .

The church itself may look very modern to the passer-by but once inside there is evidence at every turn that great care has been exercised to preserve it as much as possible in its original state. Only the stove has been removed. The building is, of course, kept locked but the key was vested with the Hawley family next door. The old brass oil lamps still adorn the walls along with a small shelf inside the door for the minister in charge to place his hat.

The pulpit is very unlike those today and several steps leading up to it give it a semblance to a very large box placed on one end. When the minister is seated he is hidden completely behind the desk from which he speaks. My attention was also drawn to a large sounding board perhaps three feet above the speaker's head — a board which would be possibly four feet square and was installed for the purpose of directing the minister's voice to the audience and not to the ceiling. I stood in the pulpit and shades of the past came before my eyes when I could see the magistrate addressing his congregation who had come to the House of God to worship — men with beards and perhaps side whiskers who had driven their horses a mile or three to be present at the Sunday service. Clothes did not make the person in those days; the women, perhaps, wore long homespun dresses and shawls over their shoulders.

As I stood in that hallowed spot I wondered what the prayer of Stephen Conger might have been after the opening of the Chapel.

A note fastened on the inside of the front cover of the old Bible gave visitors this information: This Bible is presented to the Chapel by the great great grandchildren of Arthur Youmans who is buried in this cemetery. His son, Samuel Youmans, was the father of our grandfather, Willet Casey Youmans. The son and daughter of Willet Casey Youmans, James Everett Youmans and Lena Maude Youmans were the parents of the donors.

Dora Georgina Youmans
daughter of James Everett Youmans.
Lynafred Cook Neish
daughter of Lena Maude Youmans.

A hymn book which lay beside the Bible was published in 1853 and donated by Mrs. Jane Gray in Kingston with the following note:

"I am leaving this book in memorie (sic) of my grandmother Annie Youmans who was U. E. Loyalist and was married to John Booth. When I am gone there is no one interested. In hopes someone would remember."

The Chapel has two organs — one the usual type which might be expected in any old-fashioned home but the other was the original organ installed for the dedication of the Chapel. It was manufactured by R. S. Williams & Co., Toronto, and measures three and one half feet in length, less than two in width and is approximately three feet high. The old stool accompanies it.

A framed record of the expenses in building and also the donations to the fund hangs on the walls.

There have been two marriages performed in the church during its history — Nelson B. Conger and Melissa Cronk were married in the early days of the Chapel and last fall a more modern setting was staged for the second when Archie Pearce and Kathleen Ackerman were united in the holy bonds of matrimony.

Legend has it that there was a third marriage performed in the corner of the yard but it cannot be verified. Once a man and woman were purported to have been married at midnight dressed in their night-clothes. The woman was a widow and with the death of her first husband had been left incumbered with debt. When the marriage was performed in this way no one could hold the wife responsible for any actions on the part of her previous husband.

It was with regret that I turned my back on the old Chapel with its quaint seats and its sloping gallery floor on two sides and the back.

With the gate once again locked into position and the key returned to its trustee I hoped that on my next visit the sun might be once again shedding his warmth on the scenic countryside, that the grass might be green and the flowers in full bloom. Then I could pause to include the details which had been missing from my notes on my first visit.

Roblin's Mill , rebuilt on the original cornerstone at Black Creek Pioneer Village, outside of Toronto

Roblin's Mills

Roblin's Mills in its early days was known as Way's Mills I am told, and the whole village was situated below the hill where the remains of the buildings could be seen but a few years back. It is a beautiful spot down along the mill pond but at present all that is left to remind us of former days is the epitaphs on the tombstones in the old cemetery at the foot of the hill. Here lay the remains of those to whom must be given the credit of creating the village as it was in the earlier part of the nineteenth century as well as many more who chose a resting place of peace and quietness on the edge of the body of water which saw such activity more than a century ago.

The combined enterprises of Owen Roblin contributed largely to the industrial life of the village although the largest single business was the carriage factory. But first of all let us tip-toe to the door and look in on the old mill and see how they ground their flour for it was primarily a flour mill and in its heyday Mr. Roblin used to hire teams and draw flour to Belleville and a good deal of the time wheat back to the mill. Mr. Roblin has painstakingly built the whole building as well as the stone house on the other side of the road which accounts for the flume being built across the property to carry the water to the mill. Though the stone for both buildings had been quarried from the Roblin property it was different when it came to the door-step for the house which was purchased and brought up from the farm where the Kingston penitentiary now is.

Owen Roblin, grandfather of the Roblin of our time, who always signed his name with his three initials, W. H. C., built the mill around the middle of the last century largely of stone obtained from the edge of the hill· The lumber used was mostly pine and like many of the old houses in the district, it contained boards the like of which cannot be purchased at any price today, many of them being eighteen to twenty inches in width and without the semblance of a knot.

The old mill was run entirely by water power with water brought from the lake. The raceway was dug where there was no rock and blasted where that difficulty was encountered and a wooden flume twenty-two inches square built from the southwest corner of the stone house across the road, carried the water to turn the wheels of the Roblin enterprises. The Roblin's mills included a great deal more than the old stone mill which, with its huge smokestack, speaks to the passer-by of shades of the past.

Several men were usually employed and a man by the name of Potter (no relation to the Potters at Mountain View, so far as is known) held the position of mill-wright. Steel plates like circular saws were unknown at that time so the grinding was done with two huge stones six feet across and approximately eighteen inches thick, the one at the bottom being stationary. The top stone had holes in the side so it could be lifted up with a crane and turned over to do the job which we now call changing the plates, but in those days was chipping the stones. This was a job for only an expert and had to be done at least twice a month in normal times and sometimes in the rush seasons as often as every week. The tools needed included a hammer, an assortment of chisels and a piece of board as long as the stones were wide and a can of red paint. The freshly painted board was rubbed over the stones to show up any rough spots and these were very carefully chiselled off to make the surface perfectly smooth. After this was completed grooves in both top and bottom stones were cleaned out and made sharper so that when finished they had taken on much the same patterns as the plates of today. The wheat was run through a spout to the middle and then gradually worked its way to the outside where it would be run off as a finished product.

After the water went over the wheel of the grist mill it was again used before entering the pond below, this time to drive a saw mill which was also owned by Mr. Roblin. The work was done with a perpendicular saw not unlike our present cross cut as the circular saw had not as yet come into being. The farmers drew their logs up to the west of the grist mill and unloaded them on the side of the road from where they rolled down the hill to be sawed into lumber. This slide proved great entertainment at times for the younger generation of the village and on many an occasion it was used for riding down hill, a spot which was enjoyed quite as much in those days as it is today.

The flume was open at the top for a distance of several feet inside the sidewalk before it went under the road and this was the watering place of the village. The farmers who came to get grain ground at the mill used it to water their horses providing that they had brought along their pail and housewives used the water for their weekly wash in dry times of the year. A protective railing was in evidence for many years to prevent accidents but it finally gave way to a combination of the ravages of the elements and either a farmer with a spirited team or one with a tendency to carelessness because it put up only a very faint resistance to the pressure that was exerted upon it.

When winter came, ice had formed around the opening although no one had looked upon it as dangerous. Lily Bowland was a pupil attending school at the same time as Herb Dempsey and as she wended her way through the village on the way to school, a slide on the ice looked very inviting but Lily was not quite prepared for its consequences. The ice was really slippery that morning and before a realization of what had happened came to her she was in the flume and rushing headlong toward the wheel of the mill. Her cries attracted the attention of millers in the building and, as if by miracle, Lily Bowland came out with a few sore spots but apart from near suffocation was little the worse for her experience. After that near tragedy the flume was closed and a pump put in its place.

About this time Owen Roblin decided to be a philanthropist in as far as his village was concerned. He had watched housewives carry water — some short distances and some much longer — so one day, while in a pensive mood, came to the conclusion that something should be done to alleviate this task, so he set about to provide that necessity for every household in the village. A large tank was constructed and the water was pumped by a windmill strong enough for the purpose. Pipes also of wooden construction, were laid but unfortunately the land was too shallow to permit their laying below the frost line and with the coming of winter they froze and burst and the venture had to be discarded and written off as a failure.

Only on very rare occasions was the mill ever troubled by low water and Mr. Roblin decided that some effort should also be made to remedy this situation. Accordingly, he purchased a large stationary steam engine to augment his power and built a huge smokestack of brick. The smokestack still stands and despite any fears of its crashing and causing bodily harm, it seems to have been extremely well built and unless it succumbs to destruction by mankind, its existence seems assured for still a goodly number of years. Its owner was fearful of its ability to continue to stand in its present position and last summer tried to pull it down with a large tractor, but it defied every effort, so the towering giant remains as a living memory to the man whose efforts made a village which will perpetuate the name of Roblin.

Originally the post office was Roblin's Mills, but two villages in the province by the same name were very confusing to the postal authorities and on very frequent occasions mail did not reach its proper destination and ultimate delivery was likely to be delayed for several days. To correct this situation the name of this village was changed to Ameliasburgh and Ameliasburgh it has remained.

After Mr. Roblin had completed the erection of the smokestack (it had taken two teams all one winter to draw the bricks from the village of Rednersville where they had been shipped by boat from an outside point), the water rose in the lake — he had no occasion to use it that summer nor the next, and then the business prosperity of the mills began to wane and as a result the wheels of the new motor never turned and the smokestack, which stands out as a striking example of the ingenuity and painstaking efforts of Owen Roblin, never emitted even a single puff of smoke.

The Roblin enterprises were not by any means confined to the grist mill and the one saw mill, because at the other end of the mill pond was another saw mill and an evaporator for drying apples and in between was what in those days was termed an ashery where ashes were made into lye and the lye into soap. Hardwood ashes were plentiful in those days and were collected around the country from whence they were emptied into fifty bushel hogsheads of which there were ten in number. When the soap was finished, it was drawn by team to Rednersville and shipped by boat to its destination, usually Montreal.

Excellent use of the water coming through the flume from the lake was made by Mr. Roblin. Much of the land in those days had not been cleared of its virgin stand of timber but as more settlers began to arrive on the shores of Prince Edward, more land was cleared — more trees were cut — more lumber was needed and this type of business increased to the extent where one saw was not sufficient to furnish the farmers with the lumber they needed, so a second was set up on the eastern end of the pond and the same water that drove the grist mill and the other saw mill, drove this mill also. From here it flowed off in a southeasterly direction where it eventually found its way into the marsh and so to the Bay of Quinte, but in the meantime was again used by Mirance Redner, father of our present tax collector, who ran a grist mill along the course of the water but over in the field perhaps a third of a mile south of the road which most of us know as the second concession. The family residence was close to the mill but both were eventually abandoned owing to the lack of water and another mill was erected north of the road which was run by steam. A new house was also built adjacent to the mill — the house in use at the present time.

Mr. Roblin's evaporator was situated directly down the hill from where Dr. File practised and where three of his children, Albert, Geoffrey and Luella still live. He carried on a full business of drying apples which were bought from farmers of the district. The dried fruit, bleached with a sulphur to give it a much whiter appearance, was packed in fifty pound wooden boxes for shipment and the cores and peelings shipped to United States to make jelly.

James Johnson, the watchman, gave the fire alarm one night and Geoff. and Albert File were the first ones at the scene, but flames spread so rapidly that the building was totally destroyed.

As the years came and went the saw mills also closed down and finally the grist mill. The wooden flume has also rotted and the water flow from the lake to the mill pond has been reduced to a trickle — a trickle which seeps through a crevice in the rock.

Owen Roblin was the biggest businessman in Roblin's Mills but his industries were by no means the only ones.

Sprague's carriage factory in its peak of prosperity was by far the largest single industry in the village and employed as many as fifty men at one time. The business was started by the Sprague brothers, John and Elijah, and wagons, buggies, cutters and sleighs were made as well as all kinds of custom work being done. John sold his interest to John Johnson whose father operated the farm where Clarence Vanclief now is. John married the daughter of William DeLong.

The population of the village at this time was around five hundred and Mrs. Elijah Sprague ran a boarding house having as many as twenty men at one time from the factory. It is said that she used to make cookies and doughnuts by the barrel.

Accommodation was at a premium in Roblin's Mills until Havelock DeLong built the Marsden House. This building still stands, having been used through the recent years as an apartment house.

The carriage business was conducted under the name of Sprague and Johnson for a number of years until the senior partner, Elijah Sprague, passed on and the business was disposed of to Will Hatch and Sam Allen. The former was a carriage maker while Sam Allen was a blacksmith. An old Frenchman, Peter Laveleis ran a cooperage shop where the shed is behind File's store. Sheds for tying horses, were of paramount importance in days gone by and there were three of them in Roblin's Mills — one behind the workmen building, one by the stone mill and the other at the Marsden House. Havelock DeLong did not live long to enjoy the fruits of his labours for he died the next spring after his hotel was finished and Ed. Reddick ran it for the next two years after which Jim Cook took over the management, eventually selling it to Captain Yott. The latter gained his title through sailing on the Great Lakes, mostly on a route from Kingston to Oswego where he drew huge quantities of ice besides grain and miscellaneous cargo. His home during most of his sailing years was at Rednersville in the house now occupied by Armour Reid and he often spent a day or so with his family when in the vicinity. Mrs. Yott died in the hotel and the captain spent his last years with his daughter, Mrs. Theodore Roblin, on the front road between Rednersville and Rossmore.

* * *

The first hotel on the hill could perhaps be referred to as a liquor store rather than any type of hostelry because liquor was sold in the basement of the house across the road from where the township hall now is and which was occupied for a number of years by Albert Adams.

The first hostelry was built on the grounds where St. Alban's Church now stands and the building was situated just west of the present location of the church. It was a two-storey frame building and was first kept by a man by the name of Jim Davidson. There were several families of that name residing in the township at the time but there are no available records of the relationship, if any, between this man and my wife's grandfather, who was a local preacher and who moved up to the township of Seymour some time in the sixties. All hotels in small villages had much more business than they would have today as travellers would come from the city with a "livery rig" which would be some kind of a horse-drawn vehicle, most likely a buggy, and if the business could not be completed in time an overnight stop was necessitated and of course the one place to put up was at the local hotel.

One of the best harvest days for the hotel was the one on which the local fair was held, which was usually the first Saturday in October, although the File brothers informed me that a second fair for a few years was held around the first of July, and they should be in a position to know because their father, Dr. File, besides being a medical man, was a very practical farmer and the cups still grace the shelf in the File living room which were won by the doctor with his herd of purebred Ayreshires.

On fair days the hotel shed was always full of horses and the bar was crowded with men. Liquor was enjoyed in those days quite as much as it is today and more than one person I have heard express the opinion that the open bar caused much less drunkenness than can be seen today. A man in the small village could stop and get a glass of whiskey on the way to work and, if he chose, another on the way home but now the whiskey can only be bought by the bottle or beer by the case to take home and the temptation is to just keep sipping at it until it is all used up.

Jim Davidson was followed by Jim Haley who sold out to a man by the name of Thomas Doxtator. The latter is reported to have run a wide open house and continued to serve drinks to all comers as long as the money was forthcoming. This building burned after a couple of years under the Doxtator management and Roblin's Mills was for several years without any semblance of a hotel.

With the hotel a general store was also destroyed — the store where John Sprague started his first business although he had sold out in the meantime to George Redner who was a brother of Mirance (owner of the mill and the haunted house).

I asked further information from my mother about the goings on around that house and learned that the Redners bought it from a family by the name of Drury who had built it. They had some sort of tragedy in the family — no one could be certain just what it was but the general supposition was that a young girl had been murdered — but they were sure that the ghosts of the dead returned at intervals to plague the owners of the house. On one occasion a man from Roblin's Mills, Jim Porter by name, was giving some assistance to the Redners and rather than walk the distance home he agreed to spend the night with them. Some time after midnight his bed was violently rocked and the quilts all snatched and thrown on the floor. A woman of perhaps eighteen or twenty, dressed in white, was frequently seen in different rooms of the house and on one or two occasions headless people were observed walking outside. On further questioning my mother admitted she had never seen anything although she had slept in the house when a girl but would almost take her oath that it was haunted and that repercussions from the tragic event of the past took place until finally the place was destroyed by fire.

* * *

The name of Coleman was another of importance in the early history of Roblin's Mills and David, one of the senior members of the family, ran a blacksmith shop up on the northeast corner of the crossroad from the third concession to the fourth which forms the western boundary of the village. The blacksmith business was one of utmost importance in those days and perhaps the largest part of the smithy's income was from shoeing horses. Every farmer had a driving horse and if he had a son who had an eye for romance (and few were the exceptions) he also had a sleek driving horse and a shiny buggy that could as easily as not have been made at the local carriage shop.

Then there were the farm horses which simply could not be allowed to go without shoes in the winter and if very much roading was to be done they were equipped with never slips which did not wear down so readily. (I can imagine hearing some of the younger generation inquiring, "What are never slips, Daddy?"). We used to pay a dollar to get a horse shod and if new shoes were required that was an additional dollar. Both these prices have advanced and, though I might say considerably, the price of horseshoeing today is not within the scope of my knowledge even if I do own a team. Horseshoeing, like breadmaking and even buttermaking, is rapidly becoming a lost art.

James Coleman's son, Irvine, worked with his father for some time in the blacksmith shop and then turned to undertaking and for years had a business in the village. He kept his stock in a building behind the blacksmith shop and years after he had gone out of business the barn fell a prey to fire.

I well remember Irvine Coleman and his family with whom I boarded when I first attended high school. Like the boys in the days gone by, I stayed at home until Christmas to help with the farm work — a practice which would be scoffed at today — so was at somewhat of a disadvantage when I took my first classes in the secondary school.

Joe Nightingale, who had married Letta Sprague, kept store in the building now owned by Art. Corfield on the north side of the road and almost across from the latter's home and my mother and Mrs. Nightingale were first cousins. Accordingly that made the son of the storekeeper and myself some relation but regardless of that fact both Art. Nightingale and I had been active in school fair work and likewise friends. When he started to school in the city he boarded with the Colemans who had only recently moved there from the village. After Christmas I, too lived with the same family. Irvine and Mrs. Coleman only lived in Belleville a short time after which they returned to the village from where he drew mail for some years afterward. Their only daughter, Verna married Ashton Sills and still lives in Roblin's Mills.

James Coleman's only sister married Will Kinnear, an older brother of Stuart and Thomas, and she owned a strip of land next to James and Irvine. Charles came next and owned the place where Harry Bisdee now lives, and Robert, the land where the church (United) now is and southward to the lake besides some on the north side of the road. He lived where Otis Sills now is. Then David, who was a cooper by trade, owned the land from the road to the lake where the fairgrounds were and one of his children, Isaiah was a harnessmaker for years in the village. To the east of the land owned by the Colemans came the Roblins, so it may be truthfully said that the Colemans and the Roblins at one time accounted for much of the land in the village.

George Graves lived where Clinton Sager now is and for a time ran a lime kiln from stone quarried from the edge of the hill behind the house. There were several small businesses of this nature distributed around the countryside and the fire in which wood was burned had to be kept going day and night for two weeks before the product could be called finished. Most of the lime was sold locally and at times the supply could not keep pace with the demand. Lime in those days was sold in an unslaked condition and was not hydrated as it is today.

The village for many years had a bakeshop, the first being in a building between the old Roblin flour mill and the smokestack. A man by the name of Cutts was baker and the Masonic Hall was above the bakery. Will Roblin built the Maple Leaf Bakery which was operated for many years by Frank Thompson who died in Rossmore but two or three years back.

John R. Cunningham built the old round house for the agricultural exhibits on the fairgrounds. He lived over on the other side of the lake where Milton Wood now lives. An Anglican minister by the name of Halliwell, owned the farm now occupied by Arthur Corfield and formed a partnership with Mr. Cunningham to erect a saw mill on his property on the shore of the lake. The machinery for the mill was set up by Brown's foundry in Belleville and had only commenced operations when one night Mr. Cunningham failed to return from work. The family presumed he had stayed with the File's for the night and in the morning his son, Fred, then only a small boy, came over to inquire as to the whereabouts of his father. An overturned boat told a tragic story as he always crossed the lake in the boat on the way home. No one was a witness to the accident and no reason was ever deduced for his drowning as he was looked upon as being a powerful swimmer. The lake was dragged for two days without result but on the third day Geo. Graves, on the advice of Bob Sopher, who lived on the west end of the lake, took a different course and with part of an old horserake behind his boat located the body. The mill was never operated after that. Clarence of Roblin's Mills and Harry of Rossmore are both grandsons of John R. Cunningham.

Lack of shipping facilities may eventually have become a predominant factor in the decline of the business activity of the village and then the larger centres continued to grow at the expense of the hamlets.

Roblin's Mills today has no flour mill and its one grist mill is not at present operating — it has no saw mill, no carriage factory nor bakeshop and its industrial life has been reduced to a point of non-existence.

The Village of Wellington

Early records may result in a variety of claims but from the most reliable sources of information it appears that the first white settler in Prince Edward County was Daniel Reynolds who came over from Albany, New York, and settled here in 1768. He was a trapper and fur trader and, believing that the growth of population in that district was driving the animals away, he came to Canada where he considered there might be a better chance for a successful livelihood in his chosen vocation. After a period of roaming the forests he finally decided to make his headquarters on the shores of Lake Ontario where the village of Wellington now stands.

Soon after his arrival, he constructed a crude log cabin, much to the resentment of the Indians living nearby, who did not take kindly to this invasion of their country by a white stranger. His experience as a woodsman and fur-trader soon won the friendship of the Indians and when he eventually decided to build a stone house his friend, the Indian chief named "Smoke", marshalled his fellow-tribesmen to assist.

The Manor, the oldest house in Prince Edward County, was built by the Indians under the direction of Daniel Reynolds in 1768. It is now owned and occupied by Dr. and Mrs. Garratt, the doctor being a direct descendant of the first settler.

The walls are two feet thick and built of stone carried from the lake. The mortar was made by piling limestone rock and driftwood and burning it and the large timbers were hewn by hand by the Indians. The floors are all fastened with wooden pegs. The glass, probably the first in Ontario, was brought by forest and stream from Albany, more than likely on his second trip when he returned with his wife.

The village was originally called Smokeville in honour of Daniel Reynolds and it is claimed by some that the Indians called Mr. Reynolds "Old Smoke" on account of the respect that they had for him. Others claim it was simply a nickname given him by his white neighbours in consequence of his friendship with the Indian chief of that name. Be that as it may, the village was called Smokeville in his honour for many years. After the house was sufficiently completed Reynolds returned to his home in Albany and brought back with him his bride, Nancy Waite, who, according to available records was but fifteen years old, though full of anticipation of the adventure which might lay before her in a new land.

In 1792 the Lieutenant-Governor of Upper Canada, John Graves Simcoe and party were travelling from Kingston to Newark, the then seat of government for the newly formed province of Upper Canada, when weather conditions made it impossible for further travel, so they sought shelter in the Reynolds home, which would undoubtedly be the most substantial structure in the settlement at the time. The party was entertained very hospitably in the stone house but when they prepared to depart the next morning, Lady Simcoe complained of being ill. As a consequence, their departure was delayed for a day, but it soon became evident that she was too ill to undertake any further portion of the trip and as official business pressed, the party continued their journey leaving Lady Simcoe to the kindly care of the Reynolds family. Her illness proved to be of such a nature that she was compelled to remain six weeks, during which time the Indians gathered herbs and brewed them to make medicine, and it is thought that their efforts were a contributing factor in her ultimate recovery. Daniel Reynolds owned six hundred acres of land in the vicinity and this took in a large portion of the lake front where the village now stands.

The next white settler was Isaac Garratt who came from Duchess County in New York in 1795, probably in response to one of the proclamations of Lieut.-Governor Simcoe offering land to the new settlers at a very low price. As a result, Garratt bought four hundred acres at twenty-five cents per acre. He made a clearing and began to build a house on the site where Dayton Murphy's house now stands. He was oliged to return to his family in New York State, entrusting its completion to a man who may have come over with him. But, unfortunately for him, Isaac's difficulties had only commenced.

The house had only attained the height of three logs when the man whom Isaac had left in charge was taken ill and any further construction was deferred until such time as his recovery might permit him to continue the work. In the meantime Isaac returned with his wife and six children and was greatly disappointed to find that the house was still in much the same stage of construction that he had left it and in addition, a very large tree had fallen across it. In the meantime, however, another settler by the name of Aaron White had travelled to find the little settlement and had remained in the neighbourhood. He was a man who possessed a large family but had contented himself, to begin with at least, by the erection of a very small cabin. Fortunately for Isaac Garratt, he possessed a very large heart because he took in the whole Garratt family, making them comfortable as he could until such time as their own house could be put in a condition to shelter them. The difficulty of the situation was further increased at this time by the birth of a seventh son into the Garratt family.

With the coming of Aaron White and Benjamin Garratt, brother of Isaac, Daniel Reynolds humourously remarked that he would have to move out for the pasture range on either side of him was being cut off and he was afraid he would starve.

One of the early settlers was Archibald McFaul, an Irishman of considerable fame who came here in 1815 and resided near the cranberry marsh on the town line. He shared a log house with a man by the name of Hawkes who operated a store on the site of J. Hutchinson's house. Later Mr. McFaul moved to Wellington which was still called Smokeville, and carried on business in the same place.

If there are any who might be in doubt as to how Wellington received its name, the following letter written by Dr. Benjamin Cory to *The Wellington News* in 1880, should explain it. The exact story of the naming of the village has never been definitely established although Archibald McFaul is popularly credited with choosing the name. However the letter by Dr. Cory puts a different interpretation on the matter. He states that he settled in Wellington in June, 1826, and commenced the practice of medicine there, boarding at William Garratt's, at which time the incipient village was called Smokeville and was called by that poetic name and that only, not only in the village itself but also in the country round about.

He continues:

"The article which you quote respecting the early history of Wellington is liable to lead your readers somewhat astray and among other things to the time of the establishment of the post office there and the adoption of its name as well as that of the place-names which they still retain. The article from which you quote I see at least credits my old neighbour and intimate friend Archie McFaul with having moved there in 1815.

"I came to Wellington (then Smokeville) and commenced the practice of medicine in June, 1826. In the summer of that year, I well remember having been called to Mrs. McFaul professionally when they lived out on the cranberry marsh on the township line side road. He was living in one part of a double log house and had a few goods in the other part. At this time a man by the name of Hawkes was doing a mercantile business in the store on the corner so long afterwards occupied by Mr. McFaul, who by some purchase or other arrangement became Mr. Hawkes' successor in trade and moved out 'to the front' early in 1827, his first residence in Smokeville. Mr. McFaul, ever energetic and enterprising, by his ever kind and accommodating nature, began early to do a large and increasing business. He soon saw and felt the need of a post office there and commenced agitating for it until finally in the summer of 1828, Mr. J. S. Herman, the then postmaster at Picton (the nearest place to us), through whom he had urged our claims for an office, drove Mr. Stayner, who was postmaster general at that time, up to our place to investigate the subject. My father-in-law, the late James Young, Esq., of the Carrying Place, being on a visit at the time at our place of residence, he and myself were invited over to Mr. McFaul's store to aid in discussing the matter. Mr. Stayner at once saw and admitted the propriety and necessity of a post office there. Then came up, of course, the question of its name and I well remember Mr. Young speaking up and making the suggestion that it be called Wellington. Mr. Stayner, after thinking a few minutes, said 'Yes, that will do very well, there being no post office by that name.' And so it went that the name of Smokeville, the habitation of the Indians and the earliest settlement of the white man in the county, gave way to the more modern name of Wellington — a name which it has carried all through the ensuing years."

At one time the village was the scene of much shipping, the shoreline boasting of several warehouses and at least three wharves where fleets of freight boats called on their trips up and down the lake. One point of call, known as Trumpour's dock, was situated opposite the western extremity of the main street sidewalk on the property now owned by Canadian Canners, where their branch factory No. 28 is situated. McMahon's wharf was at the foot of Narrow Street and a third, owned by Archie McFaul, was near the site of where Dr. McCullough's summer cottages have been built down the street from the post office. Loads of barley used to extend all the way from the wharf to the Belleville road when business was at its height, and farmers for miles around might be counted among those who were waiting to deliver a load of their commodity for shipment mostly to the United States.

Wellington in 1907

Archie McFaul passed on in 1864 and was buried in the cemetery beside the little church to which he gave such generous assistance during the time of its construction and to which he continued to contribute freely until the time of his death.

The church on Belleville Street was regularly used as a place of devine worship for many years. Church services were held with a degree of regularity until 1948 when, after being reduced to one a month, they were discontinued entirely as the adherents to the faith in the vicinity became fewer in number.

Besides Archie McFaul such names as Lamb, Murphy, Donovan, Kirk and Wilder may be seen on the tombstones in the burying ground — stones which are for the most part of the old type slab variety.

The village after considerable controversy, was finally incorporated in 1862. The project had been agitated for some time but was opposed somewhat strongly by the majority of the people of Hillier and to a somewhat lesser degree by the ratepayers of Hallowell. Belden's Atlas tells us that a special commission of mixed enumerators was appointed to ascertain the correctness of one condition of incorporation, that being that the population of the village had to be at least seven hundred and fifty. By 1878 the population had fallen to five hundred which may have been due in part to the fact that the fishing industry, which had flourished to such an exent, had been reduced almost to the point of extinction and a large number of people, consequently, had to seek employment elsewhere. There seems even to have been some doubt that the village actually did contain the required population when a small tract of land from the southwest corner of the Township of Hallowell and a larger one from the southeast corner of Hillier were incorporated as the Village of Wellington in a by-law of the County Council under date of October 30th, 1862. Gideon Striker as Warden, affixed his signature along with N. Ballard as clerk, and on December 20th of that year Wellington officially became a separate municipality with the right to have its own council and administer its own affairs. The first election was held at a date between December 20th and January 19th in the town hall which was afterward used as a fire hall and now as a public utilities warehouse.

* * *

One could not compile any amount of data in connection with Wellington's earlier history without making reference to the fishing industry which at one time provided a livelihood for many of its residents. From a letter written by John McCuaig, superintendent of fisheries for Upper Canada, to the Commissioner of Crown Lands, Toronto, under the date of October 16, 1857, I quote:

> The quantity caught this year, 1857, in the month of July is without precedent. In one haul in the middle of July, 47,700 fish were taken and 12,000 to 18,000 were taken in several consecutive hauls following. So great did this catch at this period, exceed any previous year, that parties engaged in fishing were found quite unprepared with salt to cure or barrels into which to pack them, in consequence, large quantities (estimate by competent

judges at least 1,500 barrels), I regret to say were lost and left to decay.

* * *

There are few villages in any district which can boast of the amount of canning factories claimed by Wellington. The first one was known as Wellington Packing Company and was constructed from an old dismantled grain elevator owned by J. Edgar Noxon at Niles Corners. It was financed by local capital from a joint stock company formed by W. P. Niles and Amos H. Baker but was eventually sold to a firm in Montreal who, in turn sold it to Canadian Canners.

The second factory, known as Lakeside Canners, was also built as a result of a joint stock company formed by Arthur Allen. Wilfred Cronk was secretary-treasurer but it too was eventually taken over as a unit of the Canadian Canners.

The third factory was built also by local capital, this one by a company organized by Harry Jolley and Edward McMahon and known as Prince Edward Canners. Harry Jolley was manager but this company was also eventually absorbed by Canadian Canners.

The next factory was known as the A. A. Morden Co. Alden Morden's parents lived not far out of the village — in Gilead, and when that gentleman looked for business expansion he purchased the Cummings' property in the edge of the village. The latter ran a tannery and owned considerable land along the Belleville Road which was known as the township line. In addition, Mr. Morden bought the holdings of a family by the name of Saylor, who owned a saw mill on the edge of West Lake· Mr. Morden operated the mill for some twenty-five years after its purchase, spending the winter and early spring sawing lumber and the summer opeating the farm. The Mordens eventually sold the canning factory to William and Keith Best who sold it to Associated Quality Canners. A disastrous fire destroyed a large portion of it but is was rebuilt and greatly enlarged. After the dissolution of the Associated Quality Canners it was purchased by Alex Lipson.

Then the Greers constructed another which was operated by four brothers, Phillip A., Charles H., Ernest and Lindley (Lyn). The latter operates the factory at the present time and is especially prominent in Rotary work while Ernest Greer and sons have a factory of their own on the lakeshore road west of the village.

Factories in the vicinity are also owned and operated by Reg. Bishop, Clare Platt and Ken Conley.

These factories, along with the local branch of Canners Seeds, Limited, provide the only phase of industrial life within the village although it might be said that fishing is an important enough industry to still be included within that category.

* * *

The prosperity of the countryside around about the village, even though it may have been bounded on the south by water, was quite in evidence by the number of blacksmith shops it contained.

On the town line, at the edge of the village, was John Rellis, who ran a general blacksmith shop and did all kinds of repair work, doing a successful business over an extended period.

ThenWright Chatterson had a shop where Albert Boyce lives.

A wood working and carriage shop was operated by Bob and Bill Boyd who afterward moved to Michigan. They manufactured buggies, wagons and sleighs and did general repair work along that line. Another shop of the same kind was operated by William Harris, grandfather of Frank, who had a ramp to put the buggies and wagons upstairs in storage.

Samuel Hyatt had a blacksmith shop where Clare Platt has his grocery store· Five blocks up the street on the same side of the road was another shop run by Henry Dunning. He also had a wood-working shop and afterward went into partnership with John Taylor. Taylor sold the business to Frank Gibson and located on a farm in the edge of Hillier village.

Today not one of the old shops is in operation in the village, their owners either having gone into different lines of business or when it came to the age of retirement, this course was followed as a natural procedure, and no one took their place as there was no business. The days of horse shoeing were no more and the small amount of repair work could be taken care of by the welding outfits in the garages.

The first bank in the village was the old Standard, which was later amalgamated with the Canadian Bank of Commerce. Then the Metropolitan Bank opened a branch at about the same time which bank was later absorbed by the Bank of Nova Scotia. As there proved to be insufficient business for both banks the field was eventually left to the Bank of Nova Scotia to which is entrusted the transaction of all money matters for not only the residents and businesses of Wellington, but the farmers round about.

The livery stable, forerunner of the modern garage, had its place too, in the early days of the village, and George Garratt ran one where Welbanks' machinery shop is now located on Wharf Street, directly behind the post office. He kept ten or twelve horses and in the heyday of business, had them all rented out most of the time. He also ran a horse-drawn bus to the station and brought the mail down as it was delivered from the train.

Harry Post ran a second stable up the street where Mrs. Graham lives, next to the Friends Church. He was a veterinary surgeon and ran the livery in connection with his other business. His premises were smaller than those of the Garratt stables and could only accommodate about half as many horses, but coupled with his work as the local veterinary, the business made a profitable sideline.

Four hotels have come and gone in the history of the village. The first in the east end on the south side of the street was known as the Brice House. This is now occupied as a dwelling, but to most of the present generation it is known as the Murphy House.

Then opposite Frank Harris' garage where Earl Marvin lives, Hugh McCullough ran the Mansion House. McCullough was a captain on the lakes, but on retirement he became another kind of captain — that of the Wellington life saving crew.

The brick house at the corner of East and Main Streets where the library now is was built by Townsend Garratt and later became known as the Wellman House, as it was run by George Wellman mostly as a summer tourist home. For years they did a thriving business and had spacious grounds with a pavilion along the lake where periodic dances were held.

Zacariah Herrington ran a hotel on the corner of West and Main for years which was known as the Herrington House. Its proprietor eventually moved to Picton and operated a hotel there by the same name. William Murphy took over the business and ran it for a time, but it is now occupied as a residence by W. E. King. Local option may have been a contributing factor in the loss of the hotels to the village but the blame for their disapperance can be laid to the changes in economic conditions. The introduction of the automobile was, perhaps, responsible most of all because with the increased distances one could travel in the course of a few hours the travellers were no longer content to remain in the smaller centres for the night.

If the advent of the automobile spelled disaster for the hotel business, just the opposite could be said of the visitors to the park which is the only public property in the village where one can go on a hot Sunday afternoon in the summer (or any other afternoon for that matter) and not only relax and eat ones lunch but enjoy the refreshing breeze as it drifts in from the waters of the lake.

* * *

The religious life of the village was looked after largely by the Quakers, the Methodists and the Anglicans after the bright star of the Roman Catholics began to dim from the loss of church membership. The first Methodist meeting house was already under way in 1833 but no records are available to tell when it was built or by whom. It did, however, stand on the property on the corner of Consecon Street now owned by William Harvey. Hitching posts were planted up and down the street for considerable distance and "Uncle Caleb" Hyatt was caretaker living next to the old church. It was sold to Lawrence Lyons in 1873 and he moved it up on the the lot where Canadian Canners office now is. It was used for some time as a carpenter's shop and dwelling house with a cheese factory in the basement run by Mr. Lyons. Eventually the buildings were demolished and the lot sold to Canadian Canners.

The lot where the present church and parsonage are situated was purchased from Ebeneezer and Daniel Reynolds on November 5th, 1857. The deed was registered on November 22nd, 1858.

Ferguson brothers were the builders and it was of brick construction with a gallery on three sides. Each pew was equipped with gates but these were disposed of in later years. The Sunday School room was at the back of the church. Rev. Thomas Jackson was the first minister and Mr. Fulton Palen (father of Mrs. Phoebe Rorabeck, who was privileged to spend a hundred years on this earth), was the first caretaker and bell-ringer. The organ was in the gallery and Mr. J. D. Day was the first organist. It was in this church that the local branch of the W.M.S. was first organized in 1891 during the pastorate of Rev. O. R. Lamly.

The church, parsonage and shed burned on November 4th, 1896, and the present church and parsonage were built the following year. During the intervening period, services were held in the Masonic hall. The pastor, Rev. J. C. Bell, occupied rooms in the house now known as Fellowship Lodge and later moved to rooms rented from Mrs. Babbit in the house where the Ogilvy family now live.

The new church was dedicated on December 5th, 1897, the dedication sermon being preached by Rev. C. Campbell. The cornerstone was laid by Dr. Platt, M.P., of Picton, on July 8th, 1897. The stone for the foundation was drawn from Allisonville and the new bell costing two hundred dollars was brought from England and donated by Isaac Minaker and W. P. Niles. It was hung on December 23rd and rung for the first time on Christmas day. For many years it was rung three times a day, morning, noon and night by Mr. Jerry Haylock to tell the time to the people of the village but this custom was discontinued with the installation of the new clock in the consolidated school.

Gilbert Dorland was instrumental in procuring the first church property for the Quakers from a man by the name of Lane, who was a large landowner in the western end of the village. In connection with the church was a cemetery most of which was used by the Quakers themselves but a small portion of it was used by the Methodists by an arrangement between the two churches. The first burial in the cemetery was that of two sailors who were drowned in Lake Ontario and their bodies washed ashore. Gilbert Dorland's wife furnished two sheets to wrap their bodies for burial.

A split came in the Quaker ranks in 1881 over certain changes in the ritual which were desired by part of the adherents to the faith. A long and bitter struggle ensued which finally resulted in a court action of which John T. Dorland and Gilbert Jones were the leaders of the opposing factions. The old or conservative Quakers being on the losing side, then built a church on the Harris property and part of the garage now occupied by Frank Harris and his son, Garratt, is the remains of this property. The present brick meeting place of the Friends (the dissenting Quakers were afterward known as Friends), is built on land purchased from Francis and Elizabeth Mitchell in 1884 and the trustees whose signatures appear on the deed are: Anthony T. Haight, Jonathan Clark Bowerman, Paul C. Haight and Elizabeth Garratt.

The history of the Anglicans goes back to about 1787 when the first missionary came to Fredericksburg in Lennox. Rev. Wm.

Macauley was the first rector of Picton and is credited, after a stiff fight, with providing the name for the town. The site upon which St. Andrew's Church in Wellington is built was purchased by an indenture drawn up on the 29th day of June, 1852, between Ebeneezer Reynolds of the Township of Hillier and Daniel Reynolds of Ogdensburgh, in the state of New York and the Church Society of the Diocese of Toronto whereby twenty-five pounds in lawful money of Canada was paid for a lot for the purpose of erecting thereon a church for the members of the United Church of England and Ireland in this province — said church to be free of taxes and assessments. The size of the land was actually three-eighths of an acre.

The education of the village dates back to the time of Archie McFaul who, so far as I could learn in the village, was the first school teacher. In those days commodities were not plentiful like they are today and it is said that both teacher and pupils attended school in the warm weather minus shoes and stockings.

Belden's Atlas disagrees with this information, however, and it says that "A man named John Stewart was the first teacher anywhere in the vicinity, but at so early a day that the exact date cannot be ascertained". Possibly there are no records available today to confirm either assertion but we can gather than Archie McFaul could not have spent much time in teaching school as he was encumbered with too many other duties including that of the first postmaster in or about 1815.

By 1876 the school had two teachers continually employed. That was in the old school behind the building which is now used for a town hall. The latter was used for years as a school until the present building was erected which serves not only Wellington Village, but a large section of the country around in the townships of Hillier and Hallowell.

The Files

The name of File is almost synonymous with the name of Roblin's Mills because, as the Roblins owned and operated the mill and the Sprague's a carriage factory, the Files farmed as a sideline but Dr. File was responsible for bringing more of the present-day citizens of Ameliasburgh Township into the world than any other resident in its history.

The Files were of U.E.L. stock and originally the family migrated from England to Holland to escape religious persecution and later came to America in or near what is now New York City. Their loyalty to the Crown, like many other residents of the thirteen states, caused them to migrate still further and the original member of their family, Malachii File with his wife and children, settled near Bath and was buried in North Fredericksburgh near the town hall.

Dr. File was born at Napanee and received his early education there, afterward attending high school at Newburg and Queen's University in Kingston. He started his first practice in Lonsdale and after a short sojourn there rode to Roblin's Mills on horseback in 1869 and started a career which gave him the distinction of making the name of Dr. File a byword in the great majority of homes in Ameliasburgh Township. He not only delivered their babies to their respective homes but doctored residents for their aches and pains and as health officer he came with the yellow and red card which served notice to the outside world that the occupants had contracted measles, fever, smallpox or whatever the case might be. Dr. Thwaite, his immediate predecessor, was an English practitioner who on passing was buried in Hillier cemetery.

On November 30, 1869, the doctor took as life partner, Catharine Barnes whose father, George Barnes, was sent out from England to manage a bank in Kingston. It was expected when the family left that country that there would be sufficient time to reach America before the birth of their child, but after a tedious six weeks passage Catharine was born two days before they landed.

Nine children of Dr. and Mrs. File grew to adulthood, the family consisting of six boys and three girls, the oldest of the boys being Fred.

The doctor and his wife, being well educated people, believed also in education for their children as four of their six sons became school teachers and their youngest son Lorne held the position of actuary for the Canada Life Assurance Co. of Toronto until his retirement.

Fred, the oldest son, received his primary education at the Roblin's Mills school after which he attended high school in Picton. On completion of his course there he attended the model school in that town and upon graduation from that institution of learning was ready to embark on a career as school teacher and his first school was at S.S. No. 10 Ameliasburgh, better known as Youngs. Our family also has a very personal interest in Youngs for some fifty odd years after, our own daughter started there in the same manner. His salary was two hundred and eighty-five dollars. Hers was twelve hundred.

After the first effort he spent two years at Albury, four at Roblin's Mills and one year at Victoria where he terminated his teaching career earning as a result of his experience the magnificent salary of four hundred dollars and by way of agreement he boarded in the section during the school days.

When the days of teaching were completed, and with a very limited capital (his savings from school teaching) he opened a small grocery store in a section of his father's office. That was in 1905 and three years later he formed a partnership with his brother Albert and the firm of File Brothers was brought into being. The business was then moved to its present location and the building was leased from a fraternal organization, the Ancient Order of United Workmen. The order was in exceedingly strong standing at that time and boasted two hundred and sixty-two members who met in the lodgerooms over the store. However membership dwindled through the ensuing years to almost nil and the building was eventually sold outright to the enterprising merchants.

During his teaching years — on October 14, 1903, Fred File was united in the holy bonds of matrimony to Clara Cunningham and has resided in Roblin's Mills since that time. Three daughters were born to the union.

The File family
From left to right: Mrs. Fred File, Fred File, Albert File

The first meeting of the township council of 1908, as one of its items of business, had to deal with the resignation of its clerk, James E. Benson. At a session under date of January 11, his son Edward was appointed temporarily until an applicant for a longer term could be located. On January 13 — two days later — at another meeting, Fred File was appointed clerk and still holds the position. His term of office may be without parallel in municipal history in Ontario.

The File family, always ardent Anglicans, were largely responsible for the building of St. Alban's Church in 1913 and Albert, the younger member of the firm, has served since that time as its sexton and its bell has been rung few times by anyone else.

During his lifetime, Fred File has never travelled too often afield. He visited Chicago for the world's fair in 1893 but "why go places to see scenery when we have a township like Ameliasburgh?" he asked. "Our township has twenty-five miles of water frontage running from Consecon and Wellers Bay to Lake Ontario and Carrying Place on the west, thence to Rednersville and Rossmore on the north along the Bay of Quinte shore, thence on the east around Massassaga completing a line almost unequalled in any municipality outside of Prince Edward. This is not taking into consideration another five miles on the south along the shore of Consecon Lake. This, and Roblin's Lake are the two inland bodies of water which tend to further beautify our township and attract visitors from the outside world".

Perhaps he has a good argument there.

Mrs. George Grey of Rednersville

Rednersville Lady of Ninety

If it were possible to go back through the files of the *Picton Gazette* to the month of March, 1847, and to find all the births recorded there as one might find them today, we would learn that on the 19th day of that month a daughter was born to Mr. and Mrs. James Brickman (nee Margaret Weese) of the front road, Ameliasburgh.

Babies have always come into the world and will, no doubt, as long as the world retains its present form, but few live to attain that ripe old age of four-score years and ten.

Such is the case, however, with Mrs. George Grey of Rednersville, who had just entered the tenth decade of her life.

I should have called on her the day of her birthday, but circumstances prevented it, so the day after I found her going about her household tasks as might be expected of a woman of twenty, yes thirty years her junior. She was glad I didn't come the day before because she had a great many callers, she said, and she realized that there were many questions I wanted to ask her so that a full measure of justice could not be done to my mission with so many interruptions.

"I went to school up at the red schoolhouse," she told me, "it was (emphasis on the was) the red schoolhouse then and a Mr. Greydon is the one teacher I remember the most of. He was a middle-aged man and boarded with his son, who lived across the road. The old schoolhouse stands today just as it did in those days with the exception of a new flagpole and a coat of grey paint, but the name of the red schoolhouse will stand as long as the building."

A story is told of a preacher named Fawcett who came along one day to inquire where the red schoolhouse was. "Right over there," answered James C. Weese to whom the question was addressed.

"But," protested the parson, "that schoolhouse isn't red,"

whereupon Mr. Weese inquired, "What colour was your buggy when it was new?"

"Why," came back the answer, "it was black."

"But it's a long way from black now," retorted Mr. Weese. So the reverend gentleman lost the argument, but the thing that really mattered was that he had found the red schoolhouse, even if it didn't happen to be so very red.

"But," I interrupted, "why should a preacher be so interested in the red schoolhouse?"

"We used to have church there," came the rely. "A crowd of young people walked up there every Wednesday eve. The preacher came down from Roblin's Mills — that was before the union of the Methodist Churches. We used to walk down to Rednersville occasionally on Sunday night but that was a Wesleyan church and we belonged to the Episcopalian, the same as the church at the Mills· The Anglicans used the hall here for a meeting place also, but the congregation dwindled, so eventually they gave it up."

I knew there were two sections of the Methodist Church, but beyond that never before had I stopped to figure out just what the division meant to the people or that at one time the churches on the compact Rednersville circuit might have had different viewpoints on religion, but such was the case.

"There was no outlet at the upper end of the bay at that time," continued Mrs. Grey, "but there was a great deal more business done then than now on the water, and a boat going from Trenton would make from four to six stops on the way to Belleville and when you wanted to spend a day in town you could go on the boat in the morning and come back in the afternoon. That was a very handy method of travelling in those days, but now — we go and are back in an hour and do quite a lot of business besides. Most of the shipping in those days was done on the boats — grain, cheese, apples and many other things that are hauled almost entirely by trucks now."

Mrs. Grey has been twice married. Her first husband was Ranseler Johnson, but he died when quite young and then she married George Grey — fifty-seven years ago.

For the most part of her life she has lived in or near Rednersville, with the exception of one year at Hilton, one at Allisonville and a short time near Mountain View, where her first husband died.

"Where did you go for a doctor in those days?" I asked.

"Oh, we always doctored with Dr. File," she told me. "I doctored with him when he first started to practise at Roblin's Mills and at one time I doctored with him for nine years steady."

"He must have done a good job," I ventured, whereupon Mrs. Kelly, Mrs. Grey's only daughter, interjected, "Mother thought she would die right away when he quit practising — but she didn't."

"He brought more babies into the world than any other doctor in his time around here and I suppose he brought yours," I suggested again.

"He was our doctor," she assured me," from the time he started out in the profession until you remember him going by with his chestnut horse taking his own time for the most part, especially on the homeward journey. He was a very familiar figure in those days, with his long flowing white beard and a ready smile for everybody."

"I suppose you lived here all through the grain boom," I asked again.

"Oh yes, but there is much more than the grain business that has disappeared with the years. A great grain business was done and that helped the whole village. Rednersville then boasted two blacksmith shops, one owned by Dave Rose and the other by Bill Urqhart."

I scratched my head. "How do you spell that?" I asked. She didn't scratch her head, but walked over to the sideboard and took out the cemetery collections book, which she has used for a great many years — a great many is the correct term, too, for there has been no family by that name here for nearly thirty years, yet the book solved the problem with little effort.

"There was at one time a grocery store on the corner where Ward's garage now is. It was run by Henry Cunningham, who," she said, "married my mother's sister. Then James Redner kept store where the store now is, and west of the Cunningham store was the village tavern. Jim Russell ran it for some time and then a man by the name of Jarvis took it over and he was running it when it burned down."

"I suppose they sold plenty of liquor in those days?"

"Well, I don't remember much about that," was the reply, "but no doubt they did because there were a great many sailors in port besides the local trade. Mercer was constable then and he ran a little store where Walter Holmes lives now. He never made many arrests that I ever heard of though".

"Isaac Snider used to run a tailor shop were the cider mill is but that is a long time ago now. We bought the house here and the old shop from William Andrew Brickman and we have made cider there for forty years. When we first started in the cider business there were few engines in the country, and we used the power that was common in those days — the old horsepower, where the horses like music now, went round and round. Many the time I have driven the team on this tiresome contraption while the apples were being ground. The pressing was always done by hand. After a few years we bought the gasoline engine and this made the work very much easier and faster. When one realizes the amount of apples that has been grown around here for a great many years it is hard to guess really how many bushels have gone through the mill but I am safe in saying that it must have been a great many indeed."

Asked as to what she attributed her long span of years, she just replied, "I have always lived a simple life, had good food and plenty of fresh air and exercise and have always liked to lend a hand to any good undertaking if I were able."

But the clock was drawing 'round, it soon would be chore time, so I shook her hand, and said, "You're good for another ten years at least," but her final comment was: "I want to stay on earth just as long as the good Lord will let me," and after all is said and done, is that not the wish of every one of us?

In Retrospect

As I pen the final article of this series I look back with a great deal of satisfaction on a season of writing which has greatly enhanced my knowledge of the history of our county and its people — a knowledge which could not possibly be obtained in any other way.

As a small beginning toward what at the time seemed to be a gigantic task, I made a mental survey which resulted in the computation of a list of fifteen men — men whom I regarded as likely prospects to tender sufficient information for at least the nucleus of a story.

The searching of records was one of the interesting items on the agenda — finding out who had lived on the place previously or who had lived there before that or to whom the land had been granted from the crown. When we consider the old world history in the light of B.C. events and the fact that the land locally was granted in the eighteenth century we have reason to wonder why our country was unkown for so long to the early European explorers.

And what changes have been brought about since the landing of the earliest settlers when John Weese spent three weeks on a trip from Adolphustown to Albury by canoe, a large part of which time was spent searching for the lone habitation of his father and mother on the south shore of the Bay of Quinte. Belden's Atlas has given considerable assistance in several instances and the only discrepancy between its records and those I have been able to uncover concerns that John Weese. I am not making mention of this fact to fault any information put forth by that atlas, but rather to make excuse for my own errors of commission or ommission because one can scarcely imagine the amount of effort concerned in collecting all the data with a view, of course, to making it as authentic as possible.

But to get back to John Weese. Belden's report says that he did not stay with his father and mother but moved across the bay and settled in Sidney Township, afterward moving farther north to about where Frankford now is. According to records in the hands of his descendants he stayed on lot eighty-nine and it was another Weese who started the settlement in Sidney. Before he passed on Randal Weese left a list of his forefathers who had lived on the farm since they had first arrived and that list included the name of John W. and his son, John. Further information along this line was given by James Francis Weese who is also a descendant of the original John W. and who related the story of the landing of John as had been told him by his father.

That story along with several others put into print during this series of articles, would in all probability never have been recorded and on the passing of our older people the door would have been closed forever.

* * *

Possibly one might make a list of life's most valuable assets — and some might even regard money as being the prime asset — but to those of us who have lived through the lean years as well as the fat, those who have been blessed with health and rewarded with many happy memories of little things we have accomplished, it would seem that a goal for money might be classed as a secondary consideration.

I was born on Ameliasburgh's second concession on the farm then owned by my grandfather Nelson Giles. We came back to the Redner farm the next year, a mile south of the village of Rednersville, and that place has been home through the years.

I received my early education in the little one-room schoolhouse at Centre and remember playing hookey on one occasion and wandering through the fields most of the day alone. Then came Belleville High School with P. C. MacLaurin as principal, and I boarded with Irvine Coleman and his wife and their daughter Verna who in later years became Mrs. Ashton Sills and served for many seasons as treasurer for the Township of Ameliasburgh. My roommate was Arthur Nightingale whose father had a general store in that village.

After graduating from High School came a course in Ontario Business College, and then came the more serious business of learning that life is largely a series of ups and downs for most people. In the "dirty thirties" I sold hogs for three dollars a hundred, six dollars for a two hundred-pounder, eggs for less than ten cents a dozen and milk for the same price per hundred pounds that we pay today for a quart. On the other end of the scale, the price of a couple of acres of land today would, in those days, have bought the whole farm of a hundred and twenty.

Always interested in writing — although the worst penman in school — I started as a correspondent for the *Picton Times* and after its printing was discontinued wrote local news for the *Gazette* in a column "From the Farm Window" and then the series of articles some of which I am presenting in this book. My old friend, Phil Dodds, who was *Gazette* editor throughout those years gave me every encouragement to publish them. The stories of Main Duck were from the store of memories of Mr. and Mrs. Wesley Thomas who kept lighthouse there for thirty-three years.

In conclusion I might say that I have not endeavoured to make this publication an authentic history of dates and data but stories which had been unfolded to me by those people I had the pleasure of interviewing, the most of whom are no longer with us. And now, after browning with age on the shelves for more than twenty years, I trust you will derive a great deal of pleasure from "It Happened in Prince Edward County".

Douglas K. Redner